BATTLE HONOURS

AWARDED FOR THE GREAT WAR.

COMPLETE LIST

The Naval & Military Press Ltd

Issued with Army Orders for February, 1925.

20
Gen. No.
5034

BATTLE HONOURS

AWARDED FOR THE GREAT WAR.

COMPLETE LIST

LONDON:
PRINTED AND PUBLISHED BY HIS MAJESTY'S STATIONERY OFFICE
To be purchased directly from H M STATIONERY OFFICE at the
following addresses: Adastral House Kingsway London W C 2;
28 Abingdon Street, London S W 1; York Street Manchester;
1 St Andrew's Crescent, Cardiff; or 120 George Street
Edinburgh; or through any Bookseller

1925

Price 6d Net

Published by

The Naval & Military Press Ltd

Unit 5 Riverside, Brambleside
Bellbrook Industrial Estate
Uckfield, East Sussex
TN22 1QQ England

Tel: +44 (0)1825 749494

www.naval-military-press.com
www.nmarchive.com

BATTLE HONOURS AWARDED FOR THE GREAT WAR

On 4 September 1922 a Special Army Order was issued approving the award of battle honours to regiments and corps of the British Army This order also directed that honours given would follow, in the Army List any that had previously been earned and should be headed by 'The Great War' and the number of battalions taking part Thus, honours earned individually by Regular, Militia (or Special Reserve), Territorial and Service Battalions were placed on one list

Throughout 1924 a number of Army Orders were issued giving the honours awarded to each regiment However, in the following year these lists were cancelled under Army Order 55 of February, and in their place a "final list" issued This list contained the honours that had been approved and directed that "no further submissions concerning the Great War battle honours will be made'

NOTE

*[The Battle Honours which have been selected to be borne on
Colours or Appointments are printed in dark type]*

**An alphabetical index of regiments
is printed at the end of the book**

By Command of the Army Council

THE WAR OFFICE,
27th February, 1925

1st LIFE GUARDS

THE GREAT WAR—2 Regiments and Household Battalion

"**Mons**," "**Le Cateau**," Retreat from Mons, "**Marne, 1914**," "**Aisne, 1914**," "**Messines, 1914**," "Armentières, 1914 ' "**Ypres, 1914, '15, '17**," "Langemarck 1914" Gheluvelt " "Nonne Bosschen, "St Julien," "Frezenberg "**Somme, 1916**," "Albert, 1916 "**Arras, 1917, '18**," "Scarpe, 1917 '18, ' "Broodseinde " "Poelcappelle,' "**Passchendaele**," "Hindenburg Line" "Cambrai 1918" "**France and Flanders, 1914–18** "

2nd LIFE GUARDS

THE GREAT WAR—2 Regiments and Household Battalion

"**Mons**," "**Le Cateau**," Retreat from Mons, Marne 1914" "**Aisne, 1914**," "**Messines, 1914**," "Armentières 1914 "**Ypres, 1914, '15, '17**," "Langemarck 1914 ' ' Gheluvelt ' ': Nonne Bosschen, ' "St. Julien ' "Frezenberg "**Somme, 1916, '18**," "Albert 1916 " "**Arras, 1917**," Scarpe 1917,' "Broodseinde '"Poelcappelle, ' Passchendaele, "Bapaume, 1918 "**Hindenburg Line**,"" Épéhy ' "**St Quentin Canal**," "Beaurevoir, ' "Cambrai 1918 "Selle "**France and Flanders, 1914–18** "

ROYAL HORSE GUARDS (THE BLUES)

THE GREAT WAR—2 Regiments and Household Battalion

Mons, "**Le Cateau**," Retreat from Mons, "**Marne, 1914**," ' Aisne 1914,' "**Messines, 1914**," "Armentières, 1914 ' "**Ypres, 1914, '15, '17**," Langemarck 1914 " "**Gheluvelt**,"" Nonne Bosschen; "St Julien " "**Frezenberg**," "**Loos**," "**Arras, 1917**," "Scarpe 1917 "Broodseinde ' ' Poelcappelle," "Passchendaele " "Hindenburg Line ' Cambrai, 1918 "**Sambre**," "**France and Flanders, 1914–18** "

1st KING'S DRAGOON GUARDS

THE GREAT WAR

"**Somme, 1916**," "**Morval**," "**France and Flanders,** 1914–17 "

THE QUEEN'S BAYS (2nd DRAGOON GUARDS)

THE GREAT WAR

" **Mons**," " **Le Cateau**," Retreat from Mons " **Marne, 1914**," " Aisne 1914," " **Messines, 1914**," ' Armentières 1914 ' " **Ypres, 1914, '15**," Frezenberg ' " Bellewaarde " " **Somme, 1916, '18**," ' Flers Courcelette " Arras 1917, " **Scarpe, 1917**," " **Cambrai, 1917, '18**," St Quentin,' Bapaume 1918 ' Rosières," " **Amiens**," Albert, 1918 " Hindenburg Line St Quentin Canal ' Beaurevoir " " **Pursuit to Mons**," " France and Flanders 1914–18

3rd DRAGOON GUARDS (PRINCE OF WALES'S)

THE GREAT WAR

" **Ypres, 1914, '15**," Nonne Bosschen, Frezenberg " **Loos**," " **Arras, 1917**," " **Scarpe, 1917**," Somme 1918 " **St Quentin**," " **Avre**," " **Amiens**," " **Hindenburg Line**," Beaurevoir ' Cambrai, 1918 ' " **Pursuit to Mons**," " **France and Flanders, 1914–18** "

4th ROYAL IRISH DRAGOON GUARDS

THE GREAT WAR

" **Mons**," " **Le Cateau**," " **Retreat from Mons**," " **Marne, 1914**," " **Aisne, 1914**," La Bassée, 1914 ' " **Messines, 1914**," " **Armentières, 1914**," " **Ypres, 1914, '15**," St Julien Frezenberg,' ' Bellewaarde,' " **Somme, 1916, '18**," ' Flers Courcelette " Arras 1917, ' Scarpe, 1917 " **Cambrai, 1917, '18**," ' St Quentin ' ' Rosières " " Amiens, " Albert, 1918 ' Hindenburg Line ' " **Pursuit to Mons**," " France and Flanders 1914–18 "

5th DRAGOON GUARDS (PRINCESS CHARLOTTE OF WALES'S)

THE GREAT WAR

" **Mons,** " " **Le Cateau,** " Retreat from Mons, " **Marne, 1914,** " " Aisne 1914,' " La Bassée, 1914 ' " **Messines, 1914,** " Armentières 1914,' " **Ypres, 1914, '15,** " ' Frezenberg " **Bellewaarde,** " " **Somme, 1916, '18,** " Flers Courcelette Arras 1917 Scarpe 1917,' " **Cambrai, 1917, '18,** " St Quentin Rosières " **Amiens,** " Albert 1918 ' Hindenburg Line St Quentin Canal, Beaurevoir " **Pursuit to Mons,** " France and Flanders 1914–18 '

THE CARABINIERS (6th DRAGOON GUARDS)

THE GREAT WAR

Mons, ' Le Cateau " **Retreat from Mons,** " " **Marne, 1914,** " " **Aisne, 1914,** " " **Messines, 1914,** " " Armentières 1914 ' " **Ypres, 1915,** " St Julien Bellewaarde,' " Arras 1917, Scarpe, 1917 " **Cambrai, 1917, '18,** " " **Somme, 1918,** " ' St Quentin, Lys ' " Hazebrouck ' " **Amiens,** " " Bapaume, 1918 " Hindenburg Line Canal du Nord Selle ' " **Sambre,** " " **France and Flanders, 1914–18** "

7th DRAGOON GUARDS (PRINCESS ROYAL'S)

THE GREAT WAR

" **La Bassée, 1914,** " " **Givenchy, 1914,** " " **Somme, 1916, '18,** " " **Bazentin,** " Flers Courcelette " **Cambrai, 1917, '18,** " " **St Quentin,** " " **Avre,** " ' Lys " Hazebrouck ' " **Amiens,** " " **Hindenburg Line,** " St Quentin Canal Beaurevoir " **Pursuit to Mons,** " France and Flanders 1914–18 '

1st THE ROYAL DRAGOONS

THE GREAT WAR

" **Ypres, 1914, '15,**" Langemarck 1914,' Gheluvelt
Nonne Bosschen ' "**Frezenberg,**" "**Loos,**" "**Arras, 1917,**"
Scarpe 1917 ' "**Somme, 1918,**" ' St Quentin " Avre
"**Amiens,**" "**Hindenburg Line,**" Beaurevoir "**Cambrai,
1918,**" "**Pursuit to Mons,**" "**France and Flanders, 1914–18**"

THE ROYAL SCOTS GREYS (2nd DRAGOONS)

THE GREAT WAR

Mons, " **Retreat from Mons,**" "**Marne, 1914,**" "**Aisne,
1914,**" ' Messines 1914, "**Ypres, 1914, '15,**" Gheluvelt '
Neuve Chapelle " St Julien, Bellewaarde "**Arras, 1917,**"
Scarpe 1917 ' Cambrai 1917 18," "**Lys,** 'Hazebrouck
"**Amiens,**" "**Somme, 1918,**" Albert, 1918 ' "**Bapaume,
1918** ' "**Hindenburg Line,**" "St Quentin Canal,' Beaurevoir "
"**Pursuit to Mons,**" "**France and Flanders, 1914–18**"

3rd THE KING'S OWN HUSSARS

THE GREAT WAR

Mons, Le Cateau "**Retreat from Mons,**" "**Marne,
1914,**" "**Aisne, 1914,**" "**Messines, 1914,**" "Armentières
1914 ' "**Ypres, 1914, '15,**" "Gheluvelt,' ' St Julien ' "Belle
waarde, "**Arras, 1917,**" Scarpe, 1917, "**Cambrai, 1917,
'18,**" "**Somme, 1918,**" St Quentin,' "Lys,' "Hazebrouck,'
"**Amiens,**" "Bapaume 1918,'" Hindenburg Line " 'Canal du
Nord " " Selle ' "Sambre " "**France and Flanders, 1914–18**"

4th QUEEN'S OWN HUSSARS

THE GREAT WAR

" **Mons,**" "**Le Cateau,**" Retreat from Mons "**Marne,
1914,**" "**Aisne, 1914,**" 'Messines 1914 ' "Armentières 1914 '
"**Ypres, 1914, '15,**" "Langemarck 1914," Gheluvelt
"**St Julien,**" 'Bellewaarde' "**Arras, 1917,**" Scarpe, 1917
"**Cambrai, 1917,**" "**Somme, 1918,**" "**Amiens,**" Hindenburg
Line Canal du Nord "Pursuit to Mons ' France and
Flanders 1914–18

5th ROYAL IRISH LANCERS

THE GREAT WAR

" **Mons,**" " **Le Cateau,**" " **Retreat from Mons,**" " **Marne, 1914,**" " **Aisne, 1914,**" " **Messines, 1914,**" " **Ypres, 1914, '15,**" " Gheluvelt, ' St Julien ' " Bellewaarde Arras 1917 Scarpe 1917, " **Cambrai, 1917,**" " Somme 1918 " **St. Quentin,**" Amiens, ' Hindenburg Line ' Canal du Nord ' " **Pursuit to Mons,**" France and Flanders 1914–18 '

THE INNISKILLINGS (6th DRAGOONS)

THE GREAT WAR

" **Somme, 1916, '18,**" " **Morval,**" " **Cambrai, 1917, '18,**" " **St Quentin,**" " **Avre,**" Lys ' Hazebrouck " " **Amiens,**" " **Hindenburg Line,**" " **St Quentin Canal,**" Beaurevoir " **Pursuit to Mons,**" " **France and Flanders, 1914–18 "**

7th QUEEN'S OWN HUSSARS

THE GREAT WAR

" **Khan Baghdadi,**" " **Sharqat,**" " **Mesopotamia, 1917–18 "**

8th KING'S ROYAL IRISH HUSSARS

THE GREAT WAR

" **Givenchy, 1914,**" " **Somme, 1916, '18,**" Bazentin, Flers Courcelette ' " **Cambrai, 1917, '18,**" ' St Quentin " " **Bapaume, 1918,**" " **Rosières,**" " **Amiens,**" " **Albert, 1918,**" Hindenburg Line ' St Quentin Canal " **Beaurevoir,**" " **Pursuit to Mons,**" " **France and Flanders, 1914–18 "**

8

9th QUEEN'S ROYAL LANCERS

THE GREAT WAR

' Mons, Le Cateau "**Retreat from Mons,**" "**Marne, 1914,**" "**Aisne, 1914,**" La Bassée, 1914,' "**Messines, 1914,**" "Armentières 1914 ' "**Ypres, 1914, '15,**" "Gravenstafel, St. Julien," ' Frezenberg " "Bellewaarde " "**Somme, 1916, '18,**" "Pozières "Flers Courcelette ' "**Arras, 1917,**" ' Scarpe 1917 " "**Cambrai, 1917, '18,**" "St Quentin "**Rosières,**" Avre, Amiens, Albert, 1918 Hindenburg Line "**Pursuit to Mons,**" "France and Flanders 1914–18

10th ROYAL HUSSARS (PRINCE OF WALES'S OWN)

THE GREAT WAR

"**Ypres, 1914, '15,**" Langemarck, 1914 Gheluvelt, Nonne Bosschen "**Frezenberg,**" "**Loos,**" "**Arras, 1917, '18,**" ' Scarpe 1917,' "**Somme, 1918,**" St Quentin ' "**Avre,**" "**Amiens,**" "**Drocourt-Quéant,**" "Hindenburg Line ' ' Beaurevoir " Cambrai 1918 " "**Pursuit to Mons,**" "**France and Flanders, 1914–18**"

11th HUSSARS (PRINCE ALBERT'S OWN)

THE GREAT WAR

Mons, "**Le Cateau,**" "**Retreat from Mons,**" "**Marne, 1914,**" "**Aisne, 1914,**" "**Messines, 1914,**" "Armentières, 1914 ' "**Ypres, 1914, '15,**" "Frezenberg ' Bellewaarde " "**Somme, 1916, '18,**" Flers Courcelette, Arras, 1917 ' Scarpe 1917, ' "**Cambrai, 1917, '18,**" St Quentin Rosières ' "**Amiens,**" "Albert 1918, ' ' Hindenburg Line ' St Quentin Canal Beaurevoir ' "Selle ' "**France and Flanders, 1914–18**"

12th ROYAL LANCERS (PRINCE OF WALES'S)

THE GREAT WAR

" **Mons,**" " **Retreat from Mons,**" " **Marne, 1914,**" " **Aisne, 1914,**" " **Messines, 1914,**" " **Ypres, 1914, '15,**" Neuve Chapelle " St Julien, Bellewaarde, " **Arras, 1917,**" " Scarpe 1917,' " **Cambrai, 1917, '18,**" " **Somme, 1918,**" St Quentin ' Lys, Hazebrouck," Amiens,' Albert, 1918 ' Hindenburg Line St Quentin Canal ' Beaurevoir " " **Sambre,**" " France and Flanders 1914–18 "

13th HUSSARS

THE GREAT WAR

" **France and Flanders, 1914–16** " " **Kut al Amara, 1917,**" " **Baghdad,**" " **Sharqat,**" " **Mesopotamia, 1916–18** "

14th KING'S HUSSARS

THE GREAT WAR

" **Tigris, 1916,**" " **Kut al Amara, 1917,**" " **Baghdad,**" " **Mesopotamia, 1915–18** " " **Persia, 1918** "

15th THE KING'S HUSSARS

THE GREAT WAR

Mons, " **Retreat from Mons,**" " **Marne, 1914,**" " **Aisne, 1914,**" " **Ypres, 1914, '15,**" ' Langemarck 1914, ' " Gheluvelt ' " Nonne Bosschen ' " Frezenberg " **Bellewaarde,**" " **Somme 1916, '18,**" Flers Courcelette " " **Cambrai, 1917, 18,**" " St Quentin," " **Rosières,**" Amiens, " Albert 1918 ' Bapaume 1918 ' ' Hindenburg Line, ' St Quentin Canal,' Beaurevoir ' " **Pursuit to Mons,**" " **France and Flanders, 1914–18** "

16th THE QUEEN'S LANCERS

THE GREAT WAR

"**Mons**," "**Le Cateau**," Retreat from Mons "**Marne, 1914**," "**Aisne, 1914**," "**Messines, 1914**," Armentières 1914 ' "**Ypres, 1914, '15**," ' Gheluvelt ' St Julien, "**Bellewaarde**," "**Arras, 1917**," Scarpe, 1917 ' "**Cambrai, 1917**," "**Somme, 1918**," Amiens,' Hindenburg Line," ' Canal du Nord ' " Pursuit to Mons "**France and Flanders 1914–18**"

17th LANCERS (DUKE OF CAMBRIDGE'S OWN)

THE GREAT WAR

"**Festubert, 1914**," "**Somme, 1916, '18**," "**Morval**," "**Cambrai, 1917, '18**," "**St Quentin**," "**Avre**," Lys, "**Hazebrouck**," "**Amiens**," Hindenburg Line St Quentin Canal,' Beaurevoir," "**Pursuit to Mons**," "**France and Flanders, 1914–18**"

18th ROYAL HUSSARS (QUEEN MARY'S OWN)

THE GREAT WAR

"**Mons**," Le Cateau Retreat from Mons "**Marne, 1914**," "**Aisne, 1914**," "La Bassée, 1914, ' "**Messines, 1914**," "Armentières, 1914 "**Ypres, 1914, '15**," "Gravenstafel St Julien '" Frezenberg "Bellewaarde "**Somme, 1916, '18**," Flers Courcelette ' Arras, 1917 ' ' Scarpe 1917 "**Cambrai, 1917, '18**," "St Quentin" "Rosières" "**Amiens**," "Albert, 1918 ' "**Hindenburg Line**," Pursuit to Mons "**France and Flanders, 1914–18**"

19th ROYAL HUSSARS (QUEEN ALEXANDRA'S OWN)

THE GREAT WAR

"**Le Cateau**," "**Retreat from Mons**," "**Marne, 1914**," "**Aisne, 1914**," "**Armentières, 1914**," "**Ypres, 1915**," Frezenberg ' Bellewaarde, "**Somme, 1916, '18**," Flers Courcelette," "**Cambrai, 1917, '18**," "St Quentin '' Rosières ' "**Amiens**," Albert 1918,' Bapaume 1918 ' Hindenburg Line St Quentin Canal,' ' Beaurevoir "**Pursuit to Mons**," " France and Flanders 1914–18

20th HUSSARS

THE GREAT WAR

" Mons," " Retreat from Mons," " Marne, 1914," " Aisne, 1914," " Messines, 1914," " Ypres, 1914, '15," Neuve Chapelle " St Julien, " Bellewaarde Arras 1917, ' Scarpe, 1917 " **" Cambrai, 1917, '18," " Somme, 1918,"** ' St Quentin " Lys, Hazebrouck, **" Amiens,"** " Albert 1918, ' Bapaume, 1918 ' Hindenburg Line, ' " St Quentin Canal " ' Beaurevoir " **" Sambre,"** " France and Flanders 1914–18 "

21st LANCERS (EMPRESS OF INDIA'S)

THE GREAT WAR

" N W Frontier India, 1915, '16 "

NORTH IRISH HORSE

THE GREAT WAR

" Retreat from Mons," " Marne, 1914," " Aisne, 1914," " Armentières, 1914," Somme, 1916, 18 **" Albert, 1916," " Messines, 1917," " Ypres, 1917,"** Pilckem " St. Quentin, **" Bapaume, 1918,"** Hindenburg Line " " Épéhy, " St Quentin Canal **" Cambrai, 1918," " Selle,"** Sambre ' France and Flanders 1914–18

SOUTH IRISH HORSE

THE GREAT WAR

" Loos," " Somme, 1916, '18," " Albert, 1916," " St. Quentin," " Rosières," " Avre," " Ypres, 1918," " Courtrai," " France and Flanders, 1915–18 "

KING EDWARD'S HORSE (THE KING'S OVERSEA DOMINIONS REGIMENT)

THE GREAT WAR

" Loos," " Ypres, 1917," " Pilckem," " Cambrai, 1917," " Lys," " Estaires," " Hazebrouck," " Pursuit to Mons," " France and Flanders, 1915–17, 1918 " " Italy, 1917–18 "

THE AYRSHIRE YEOMANRY (EARL OF CARRICK'S OWN) (HUSSARS)

THE GREAT WAR

" Ypres, 1918," " France and Flanders, 1918." " Gallipoli, 1915 " " Rumani," " Egypt, 1916–17 " " Gaza," " Jerusalem," " Tell 'Asur," " Palestine, 1917–18 "

BEDFORDSHIRE YEOMANRY (LANCERS)

THE GREAT WAR

" Somme, 1916, '18," " Flers-Courcelette," " Cambrai, 1917," " France and Flanders, 1915–18 "

BERKS YEOMANRY (HUNGERFORD) (DRAGOONS)

THE GREAT WAR

" Arras, 1918," Scarpe, 1918, " Ypres, 1918," Courtrai " France and Flanders, 1918 " " Suvla," " Scimitar Hill," " Gallipoli, 1915 " " Egypt, 1915–17 " " Gaza," " El Mughar," Nebi Samwil ' " Palestine, 1917–18 "

BUCKINGHAMSHIRE YEOMANRY (ROYAL BUCKS HUSSARS)

THE GREAT WAR

" Arras, 1918," " Scarpe, 1918," " Ypres, 1918," Courtrai " France and Flanders, 1918 " Suvla, " Scimitar Hill," " Gallipoli, 1915." " Egypt, 1915–17." " Gaza," " El Mughar," ' Nebi Samwil ' " Palestine, 1917–18 "

THE CHESHIRE YEOMANRY (EARL OF CHESTER'S) (HUSSARS)

THE GREAT WAR

" Somme, 1918," " Bapaume, 1918," " Hindenburg Line,"
" Épéhy," " Pursuit to Mons," " France and Flanders, 1918 "
Egypt 1916–17. " Gaza," " Jerusalem," " Jericho,"
" Tell 'Asur," ' Palestine 1917–18

DENBIGHSHIRE YEOMANRY (HUSSARS)

THE GREAT WAR

" Ypres, 1918," " France and Flanders, 1918." " Egypt,
1916–17." " Gaza," "Jerusalem," "Jericho," "Tell 'Asur,"
" Palestine, 1917–18 "

DERBYSHIRE YEOMANRY (DRAGOONS)

THE GREAT WAR

" Struma," " Macedonia, 1916–18 " " Suvla," " Scimitar
Hill," " Gallipoli, 1915 " " Egypt, 1915–16 "

ROYAL 1st DEVON YEOMANRY (HUSSARS)

THE GREAT WAR

" Somme, 1918," " Bapaume, 1918," " Hindenburg Line,"
" Épéhy," Pursuit to Mons " France and Flanders, 1918 "
" Gallipoli, 1915 " " Egypt, 1916–17." " Gaza," "Jeru-
salem," " Tell Asur " Palestine, 1917–18 "

ROYAL NORTH DEVON YEOMANRY (HUSSARS)

THE GREAT WAR

" Somme, 1918," " Bapaume, 1918," " Hindenburg Line,"
" Épéhy," Pursuit to Mons, " France and Flanders, 1918 "
" Gallipoli, 1915 " " Egypt, 1916 – 17." " Gaza,"
" Jerusalem," ' Tell Asur " Palestine, 1917–18 "

DORSET YEOMANRY (QUEEN'S OWN)

THE GREAT WAR

" Suvla," " Scimitar Hill," " Gallipoli, 1915 " " Agagiya,"
" Egypt, 1915–17 " " Gaza," " El Mughar," " Nebi Samwil,"
Megiddo ' " Sharon   " Damasous," " Palestine, 1917–18 "

ESSEX YEOMANRY (DRAGOONS)

THE GREAT WAR

" Ypres, 1915," " St Julien," " Frezenberg," " Loos,"
" Arras, 1917," " Scarpe, 1917," " Somme, 1918," " France
and Flanders, 1914–18 "

FIFE AND FORFAR YEOMANRY

THE GREAT WAR

" Somme, 1918," " Bapaume, 1918," " Hindenburg Line,"
" Épéhy,"   Pursuit to Mons   " France and Flanders, 1918 "
" Gallipoli, 1915 " " Egypt, 1915–17 " " Gaza," " Jeru-
salem," " Tell Asur   " Palestine, 1917–18 "

GLAMORGAN YEOMANRY (DRAGOONS)

THE GREAT WAR

Somme 1918   Bapaume 1918   " Hindenburg Line,"
" Épéhy," " Pursuit to Mons," " France and Flanders,
1918 " " Egypt, 1916–17 "   " Gaza,"   " Jerusalem,"
" Jericho," " Tell 'Asur," " Palestine, 1917–18 "

GLOUCESTERSHIRE YEOMANRY (ROYAL GLOUCESTERSHIRE HUSSARS)

THE GREAT WAR

" Suvla," Scimitar Hill, " Gallipoli, 1915 " " Rumani," " Rafah," " Egypt, 1915–17 " " Gaza," " El Mughai " " Nebi Samwil " " Jerusalem," " Megiddo," " Sharon ' " Damascus," " Palestine, 1917–18 "

HAMPSHIRE (CARABINIERS) (DRAGOONS)

THE GREAT WAR

" Messines, 1917," " Somme, 1918," " St Quentin," " Bapaume, 1918," " Arras, 1918," " Ypres, 1918," " Courtrai," " France and Flanders, 1916–17, 1918 " " Italy, 1917–18 "

HERTS YEOMANRY (DRAGOONS)

THE GREAT WAR

" Suvla," " Scimitar Hill," " Gallipoli, 1915 " " Suez Canal," " Egypt, 1915–16 " " Megiddo," " Sharon," " Damascus," " Palestine, 1918 "

ROYAL EAST KENT YEOMANRY (THE DUKE OF CONNAUGHT'S OWN) (MOUNTED RIFLES) (HUSSARS)

THE GREAT WAR

" Somme, 1918," " Bapaume, 1918," " Hindenburg Line," " Épéhy," " Pursuit to Mons," " France and Flanders, 1918 " " Gallipoli, 1915 " " Egypt, 1916–17 " " Gaza," " Jerusalem " " Tell 'Asur ' " Palestine, 1917–18 "

WEST KENT YEOMANRY (QUEEN'S OWN) (HUSSARS)

THE GREAT WAR

" Somme, 1918," " Bapaume, 1918," " Hindenburg Line,"
" Épéhy," " Pursuit to Mons," " France and Flanders,
1918 " "Gallipoli, 1915 " " Egypt, 1916–17." " Gaza,"
" Jerusalem " " Tell 'Asur ' " Palestine, 1917–18 "

THE LANARKSHIRE YEOMANRY (LANCERS)

THE GREAT WAR

" Ypres, 1918," " France and Flanders, 1918 " " Gallipoli,
1915 " " Egypt, 1916–17 " " Gaza," " Jerusalem," " Tell
'Asur," " Palestine, 1917 18 "

QUEEN'S OWN ROYAL GLASGOW YEOMANRY (DRAGOONS)

THE GREAT WAR

" Loos," " Ypres, 1917, '18," " Passchendaele," " Somme,
1918," " Bapaume, 1918," " Ancre, 1918," " Courtrai,"
" France and Flanders, 1915–18 "

THE LANCASHIRE HUSSARS YEOMANRY

THE GREAT WAR

" Somme, 1916, '18," " Albert, 1916," " Ypres, 1917,"
" Pilckem," " St Quentin," " Rosières," Lys " " Kemmel,"
Scherpenberg " Hindenburg Line," " Cambrai, 1918,"
Selle " " France and Flanders, 1916–18 "

THE DUKE OF LANCASTER'S OWN YEOMANRY (DRAGOONS)

THE GREAT WAR

" Somme, 1916, '18," " Albert, 1916, '18," " Ypres, 1917,"
" Passchendaele," " St Quentin," ' Bapaume, 1918
" Amiens," " Hindenburg Line," ' Épéhy," " Cambrai,
1918," " Selle " Sambre," " France and Flanders, 1915–18 "

THE LEICESTERSHIRE YEOMANRY (PRINCE ALBERT'S OWN) (HUSSARS)

THE GREAT WAR

" Ypres, 1914, '15," " St. Julien," " Frezenberg," " Arras,
1917," " Scarpe, 1917," " France and Flanders, 1914–18 "

LINCOLNSHIRE YEOMANRY (LANCERS)

THE GREAT WAR

" Selle," " Valenciennes," " Sambre," " France and
Flanders, 1918." " Egypt, 1915–17," " Gaza," " El Mughar,"
" Nebi Samwil," " Palestine, 1917–18 "

CITY OF LONDON YEOMANRY (ROUGH RIDERS) (LANCERS)

THE GREAT WAR

" Pursuit to Mons," " France and Flanders, 1918 "
" Macedonia, 1916–17 " " Suvla," " Scimitar Hill,"
" Gallipoli, 1915 " " Rumani," " Egypt 1915–16 " " Gaza,"
El Mughar ' " Nebi Samwil," " Palestine, 1917–18 "

1st COUNTY OF LONDON YEOMANRY (MIDDLESEX, DUKE OF CAMBRIDGE'S HUSSARS)

THE GREAT WAR

" Macedonia, 1916–17." " Suvla," " Scimitar Hill,"
" Gallipoli, 1915 " " Egypt, 1915–16 " Gaza," " El
Mughar ' " Nebi Samwil," " Megiddo," " Sharon,"
" Damascus," " Palestine, 1917–18 "

2nd COUNTY OF LONDON YEOMANRY (WESTMINSTER DRAGOONS)

THE GREAT WAR

" Courtrai," " France and Flanders, 1918 " " Suvla,"
" Scimitar Hill," " Gallipoli, 1915 " " Suez Canal," " Egypt,
1915–17 " " Gaza," " El Mughar ' " Jerusalem," " Palestine,
1917–18 "

3rd COUNTY OF LONDON YEOMANRY (SHARPSHOOTERS) (HUSSARS)

THE GREAT WAR

" Pursuit to Mons," " France and Flanders, 1918 "
" Macedonia, 1916–17 " Suvla ' " Scimitar Hill," " Galli-
poli, 1915 " " Egypt, 1915–16." " Gaza," " El Mughar,"
" Nebi Samwil," " Palestine, 1917–18 "

LOTHIANS AND BORDER HORSE (DRAGOONS)

THE GREAT WAR

" France and Flanders, 1915 " " Doiran, 1918," " Macedonia, 1915–18 "

THE LOVAT SCOUTS

THE GREAT WAR—2 Regiments

" France and Flanders, 1916–18."   " Macedonia, 1916–18 "
" Gallipoli, 1915 "   " Egypt, 1915–16 "

MONTGOMERYSHIRE YEOMANRY (DRAGOONS)

THE GREAT WAR

" Somme, 1918," " Bapaume, 1918," " Hindenburg Line,"
" Épéhy," " Pursuit to Mons " " France and Flanders, 1918 "
" Egypt, 1916–17 "   " Gaza," " Jerusalem," " Jericho,"
Tell 'Asur " " Palestine, 1917–18 "

NORFOLK YEOMANRY (THE KING'S OWN ROYAL REGIMENT) (DRAGOONS)

THE GREAT WAR

" Ypres, 1918," " France and Flanders, 1918 " " Gallipoli,
1915 " " Egypt, 1915–17 " " Gaza," " Jerusalem," " Tell
'Asur," " Palestine, 1917–18 "

NORTHAMPTONSHIRE YEOMANRY (DRAGOONS)

THE GREAT WAR

" Neuve Chapelle," " Ypres, 1915," " Arras, 1917,"
" Scarpe, 1917," " France and Flanders, 1914–17 " " Vittorio
Veneto," " Italy, 1917–18 "

THE NORTHUMBERLAND HUSSARS (YEOMANRY)

THE GREAT WAR

" Ypres, 1914," " Langemarck, 1914," " Gheluvelt,"
" Neuve Chapelle," " Loos," " Cambrai, 1917," " Somme,
1918," ' St Quentin " Albert, 1918," " Selle ' " Sambre,"
" France and Flanders, 1914–18 "

THE NOTTINGHAMSHIRE YEOMANRY (SHERWOOD RANGERS) (HUSSARS)

THE GREAT WAR

Struma, "**Macedonia, 1916–17**" "**Suvla,**" "**Scimitar Hill,**" "**Gallipoli, 1915**" "**Egypt, 1915–16**" "**Gaza,**" "**El Mughar**" "**Nebi Samwil,**" "**Megiddo,**" Sharon "**Damascus,**" "**Palestine, 1917–18**"

NOTTINGHAMSHIRE YEOMANRY (SOUTH NOTTINGHAMSHIRE HUSSARS)

THE GREAT WAR

"**Hindenburg Line,**" "**Épéhy,**" St Quentin Canal Beaurevoir, ' "**Selle,**" "**Sambre,**" France and Flanders, 1918." "**Struma,**" Macedonia, 1916–17 "**Suvla,**" "**Scimitar Hill,**" Gallipoli, 1915. Egypt 1915–16 "**Gaza,**" "**El Mughar,**" "**Nebi Samwil,**" Palestine 1917–18

OXFORDSHIRE YEOMANRY (QUEEN'S OWN OXFORDSHIRE HUSSARS)

THE GREAT WAR

"**Messines, 1914,**" "**Armentières, 1914,**" "**Ypres, 1915,**" St Julien, ' "**Bellewaarde** ' "**Arras, 1917,**" Scarpe 1917 "**Cambrai, 1917, '18,**" "**Somme, 1918,**" St Quentin "**Lys,**" ' Hazebrouck, "**Amiens,**" Bapaume, 1918 "**Hindenburg Line,**" "Canal du Nord Selle " "Sambre "**France and Flanders, 1914–18**"

PEMBROKE YEOMANRY (CASTLEMARTIN) (HUSSARS)

THE GREAT WAR

Somme 1918 Bapaume 1918 "**Hindenburg Line,**" "**Épéhy,**" "**Pursuit to Mons,**" "**France and Flanders, 1918**" "**Egypt, 1916–17**" "**Gaza,**" "**Jerusalem,**" "**Jericho,**" "**Tell 'Asur,**" "**Palestine, 1917–18**"

THE SCOTTISH HORSE

THE GREAT WAR

"Hindenburg Line," "St Quentin Canal," Cambrai, 1918 ' "Beaurevoir," "Selle," "Sambre," "France and Flanders, 1918 " "Macedonia, 1916–18 " "Gallipoli, 1915 " "Rumani," "Egypt, 1915–16 "

SHROPSHIRE YEOMANRY (DRAGOONS)

THE GREAT WAR

"Somme, 1918," "Bapaume, 1918," "Hindenburg Line," "Épéhy," Pursuit to Mons, "France and Flanders, 1918 " "Egypt, 1916–17 " "Gaza," "Jerusalem," Jericho ' "Tell 'Asur," "Palestine, 1917–18 "

THE NORTH SOMERSET YEOMANRY (DRAGOONS).

THE GREAT WAR

"Ypres, 1914, '15," "Frezenberg," "Loos," "Arras, 1917," "Scarpe, 1917," "France and Flanders, 1914–18 "

WEST SOMERSET YEOMANRY (HUSSARS)

THE GREAT WAR

"Somme, 1918," Bapaume 1918 "Hindenburg Line," "Épéhy," "Pursuit to Mons," "France and Flanders, 1918 " "Gallipoli, 1915." "Egypt, 1916–17 " "Gaza," "Jerusalem," 'Tell Asur ' "Palestine, 1917–18 "

THE STAFFORDSHIRE YEOMANRY (QUEEN'S OWN ROYAL REGIMENT) (HUSSARS)

THE GREAT WAR

" Egypt, 1915–17 "   " Gaza,"   " El Mughar,"   " Nebi Samwil,"" Megiddo,"" Sharon,"" Damascus,"" Palestine, 1917–18 "

SUFFOLK YEOMANRY (THE DUKE OF YORK'S OWN LOYAL SUFFOLK HUSSARS)

THE GREAT WAR

" Somme, 1918," " Bapaume, 1918," " Hindenburg Line," " Épehy," " Pursuit to Mons," " France and Flanders, 1918 " " Gallipoli, 1915 "   " Egypt, 1915–17 "   " Gaza," " Jerusalem," ' Tell Asur   "Palestine 1917–18

SURREY YEOMANRY (QUEEN MARY'S REGIMENT) (LANCERS)

THE GREAT WAR

"Ypres, 1915," "France and Flanders, 1915 "   " Struma," " Macedonia, 1916–18 "   " Egypt, 1915 "

SUSSEX YEOMANRY (DRAGOONS)

THE GREAT WAR

" Somme, 1918," " Bapaume, 1918," " Hindenburg Line," " Épehy," " Pursuit to Mons," France and Flanders, 1918 " Gallipoli, 1915 "   " Egypt, 1916–17." " Gaza," " Jerusalem," " Tell 'Asur," "Palestine 1917–18

THE WARWICKSHIRE YEOMANRY (HUSSARS)

THE GREAT WAR

"Hindenburg Line," Épéhy "St Quentin Canal," Beaurevoir, ' "Selle, "Sambre," "France and Flanders, 1918 " ' Suvla, ' "Scimitar Hill," "Gallipoli, 1915 " "Rumani, "Rafah," "Egypt, 1915–17." "Gaza," El Mughar ̗ Nebi Samwil " 'Jerusalem ' "Palestine, 1917–18 "

WELSH HORSE (LANCERS)

THE GREAT WAR

"Somme, 1918," Bapaume 1918 "Hindenburg Line," Épéhy " "Pursuit to Mons," "France and Flanders, 1918 " "Gallipoli, 1915 " "Egypt, 1915–17." "Gaza," "Jerusalem," "Jericho," Tell 'Asur "Palestine, 1917–18 "

WESTMORLAND AND CUMBERLAND YEOMANRY (HUSSARS)

THE GREAT WAR

"Ypres, 1917," "Poelcappelle," "Passchendaele," "Somme, 1918," St Quentin ' "Bapaume 1918 ' "Amiens," Albert, 1918 "Hindenburg Line," "Épéhy," "Cambrai, 1918," ' Selle "Sambre," "France and Flanders, 1915–18 "

THE ROYAL WILTSHIRE YEOMANRY (PRINCE OF WALES'S OWN) (HUSSARS)

THE GREAT WAR

"Ypres, 1917," Polygon Wood "Broodseinde," Poel cappelle " ' Passchendaele ' "Somme, 1918," "St Quentin," "Bapaume, 1918," "Lys," "Messines, 1918," "Bailleul," "Kemmel," "France and Flanders, 1916–18 "

WORCESTERSHIRE YEOMANRY (THE QUEEN'S OWN WORCESTERSHIRE HUSSARS)

THE GREAT WAR

"Suvla," Scimitar Hill, "Gallipoli, 1915," "Rumani," "Rafah," "Egypt, 1915–17" "Gaza," "El Mughar" "Nebi Samwil" "Jerusalem," "Megiddo," "Nablus" "Damascus," "Palestine, 1917–18"

THE YORKSHIRE DRAGOONS YEOMANRY (QUEEN'S OWN)

THE GREAT WAR

"Cambrai, 1917," "Courtrai," "France and Flanders, 1915–18"

THE YORKSHIRE HUSSARS YEOMANRY (ALEXANDRA, PRINCESS OF WALES'S OWN)

THE GREAT WAR

"Arras, 1918," "Scarpe, 1918," "Drocourt–Quéant," "Hindenburg Line," "Canal du Nord," "Cambrai, 1918," "Selle," "Valenciennes," "Sambre," "France and Flanders, 1915–18"

EAST RIDING OF YORKSHIRE YEOMANRY (LANCERS)

THE GREAT WAR

"Selle," "Valenciennes," "Sambre," "France and Flanders, 1918" "Egypt, 1915–17" "Gaza," "El Mughar," "Nebi Samwil," "Palestine, 1917–18"

HONOURABLE ARTILLERY COMPANY

THE GREAT WAR—3 Infantry Battalions and 7 Batteries
of Artillery

"Ypres, 1915, '17," "Somme, 1916, '18," Ancre Heights
"Ancre, 1916," "Arras, 1917, '18," ' Scarpe 1917, '18
Arleux ' **"Bullecourt,"** ' Pilckem ' Polygon Wood ' ' Brood
seinde, Poelcappelle " **"Passchendaele,"** " Amiens, Albert
1918 " Bapaume, 1918 ' Drocourt Quéant " "Hindenburg
Line Épéhy,' ' St Quentin Canal ' Cambrai, 1918 ' Selle "
" Sambre " **"France and Flanders, 1914–18 "** Piave
"Vittorio Veneto," ' Italy 1917–18. ' Rafah, Egypt,
1915–17 ' **"Gaza,"** El Mughar **"Jerusalem,"** Jordan "
' Megiddo " Sharon Damascus ' Palestine 1917–18
Aden "

GRENADIER GUARDS

THE GREAT WAR—5 Battalions

Mons, Retreat from Mons **" Marne, 1914," " Aisne,
1914," " Ypres, 1914, '17,"** " Langemarck, 1914 " " Gheluvelt '
" Nonne Bosschen ' " Neuve Chapelle," " Aubers ' Festubert
1915 ' **" Loos," " Somme, 1916, '18,"** " Ginchy, ' " Flers
Courcelette ' Morval " " Pilckem Menin Road, ' Poel-
cappelle " Passchendaele ' **" Cambrai, 1917, '18,"**
' St Quentin, " Bapaume, 1918, **" Arras, 1918,"** ' Lys
" Hazebrouck," Albert, 1918 ' " Scarpe 1918, **" Hindenburg
Line,"** ' Havrincourt ' " Canal du Nord ' " Selle " " Sambre "
" France and Flanders, 1914–18 "

COLDSTREAM GUARDS

THE GREAT WAR—5 Battalions

Mons **" Retreat from Mons," " Marne, 1914," " Aisne,
1914," " Ypres, 1914, '17,"** ' Langemarck 1914 ' " Gheluvelt '
Nonne Bosschen Givenchy 1914 ' ' Neuve Chapelle
Aubers ' Festubert, 1915 ' **" Loos,"** ' Mount Sorrel
" Somme, 1916, '18," ' Flers Courcelette, ' " Morval
Pilckem ' ' Menin Road Poelcappelle ' ' Passchendaele
" Cambrai, 1917, '18," St Quentin, Bapaume 1918
" Arras, 1918," Lys **" Hazebrouck,"** " Albert 1918 '
Scarpe 1918,' Drocourt Quéant ' **" Hindenburg Line,"**
Havrincourt " Canal du Nord ' Selle ' " Sambre ' France
and Flanders 1914–18 '

SCOTS GUARDS

THE GREAT WAR—3 Battalions

"Retreat from Mons," "Marne, 1914," "Aisne, 1914," "Ypres, 1914, '17," ' Langemarck, 1914 ' "Gheluvelt, 'Nonne Bosschen Givenchy, 1914,' "Neuve Chapelle,' ' Aubers ' **"Festubert, 1915," "Loos," "Somme, 1916, '18,"** " Flers Courcelette," "Morval, "Pilckem,' "Poelcappelle 'Passchendaele,' **"Cambrai, 1917, '18,"** St Quentin ' "Albert, 1918 ' "Bapaume 1918, 'Arras 1918, Drocourt Quéant **"Hindenburg Line,"** ' Havrincourt " Canal du Nord "Selle ' Sambre ' **"France and Flanders, 1914–18 "**

IRISH GUARDS

THE GREAT WAR—3 Battalions

Mons, **"Retreat from Mons," "Marne, 1914," "Aisne, 1914," "Ypres, 1914, '17,"** ' Langemarck, 1914 ' "Gheluvelt ' "Nonne Bosschen ' **"Festubert, 1915," "Loos," "Somme, 1916, '18,"** " Flers Courcelette ' Morval, 'Pilckem, "Poel cappelle ' Passchendaele ' **"Cambrai, 1917, '18,"** St Quentin Lys ' **"Hazebrouck,"** ' Albert 1918 "Bapaume, 1918 ' Arras 1918, Scarpe 1918,' Drocourt Quéant " **"Hindenburg Line,"** Canal du Nord Selle ' "Sambre ' France and Flanders 1914–18

WELSH GUARDS

THE GREAT WAR—2 Battalions

"Loos," Somme, 1916, 18 **"Ginchy," "Flers-Courcelette," "Morval,"** "Ypres 1917, **"Pilckem," "Poelcappelle," "Passchendaele," "Cambrai, 1917, '18," "Bapaume, 1918,"** Arras, 1918 ' Albert, 1918 ' "Drocourt Quéant ' "Hindenburg Line ' Havrincourt ' **"Canal du Nord,"** "Selle **"Sambre,"** France and Flanders 1915–18

THE ROYAL SCOTS (THE ROYAL REGIMENT)

THE GREAT WAR—35 Battalions

Mons, "**Le Cateau,**" Retreat from Mons "**Marne, 1914, '18,**" Aisne, 1914" La Bassée 1914,' "Neuve Chapelle' "**Ypres, 1915, '17, '18,**" "Gravenstafel "St Julien Frezenberg,' 'Bellewaarde, Aubers' "Festubert 1915 "**Loos,**" "**Somme, 1916, '18,**" Albert 1916, '18, "Bazentin Pozières, "Flers Courcelette' Le Transloy,' 'Ancre Heights Ancre 1916, '18 "**Arras, 1917, '18,**" "Scarpe 1917, '18 Arleux' "Pilckem "Langemarck, 1917 "Menin Road 'Polygon Wood Poelcappelle "Passchendaele "Cambrai 1917' "St Quentin' Rosières,' "**Lys,**" "Estaires 'Messines, 1918 'Hazebrouck, "Bailleul' "Kemmel," Béthune" "Soissonnais Ourcq," 'Tardenois" Amiens" "Bapaume 1918 Drocourt Quéant,' Hindenburg Line" Canal du Nord St Quentin Canal' 'Beaurevoir" Courtrai,' Selle, Sambre' "France and Flanders 1914–18 "**Struma,**" "Macedonia 1915–18' 'Helles," "Landing at Helles, "Krithia Suvla,' "Scimitar Hill' "**Gallipoli, 1915–16**" Rumani Egypt, 1915–16" "Gaza, El Mughar, 'Nebi Samwil Jaffa" "**Palestine, 1917–18**" 'Archangel 1918–19

THE QUEEN'S ROYAL REGIMENT (WEST SURREY)

THE GREAT WAR—25 Battalions

Mons, "**Retreat from Mons,**" Marne 1914 18, Aisne, 1914' "**Ypres, 1914, '17, '18,**" "Langemarck 1914" "Gheluvelt, ' 'Aubers ' Festubert, 1915, "Loos' "**Somme, 1916, '18,**" Albert 1916 '18 ' 'Bazentin "Delville Wood' "Pozières,' "Guillemont Flers Courcelette' 'Morval, Thiepval Le Transloy Ancre Heights Ancre 1916 '18," "Arras, 1917 18,' "Scarpe 1917" 'Bullecourt "**Messines, 1917,**" "Pilckem' "Menin Road" Polygon Wood' "Brood scinde Passchendaele' "Cambrai 1917 '18, 'St Quentin' "Bapaume, 1918" "Rosières, "Avre" Villers Bretonneux Lys' "Hazebrouck,' Bailleul, 'Kemmel "Soissonnais Ourcq, Amiens' "**Hindenburg Line,**" "Épéhy St. Quentin Canal' Courtrai "Selle,' "Sambre France and Flanders, 1914–18. "Piave "**Vittorio Veneto,**" "Italy, 1917–18." 'Suvla." Landing at Suvla' Scimitar Hill," "**Gallipoli, 1915**" Rumani" 'Egypt, 1915–16.' "Gaza' El Mughar" "Jerusalem,' "Jericho" "Tell 'Asur,' "**Palestine, 1917–18**" 'Khan Baghdadi," "**Mesopotamia, 1915–18**" "**N W Frontier India, 1916–17**"

THE BUFFS (EAST KENT REGIMENT)

THE GREAT WAR—16 Battalions

Aisne 1914, "**Armentières, 1914**," "**Ypres, 1915, '17,**" Gravenstafel,' St Julien ' Frezenberg,' "Bellewaarde Hooge, 1915, "**Loos**," "**Somme, 1916, '18,**" "Albert 1916 '18, "Bazentin,' ' Delville Wood,' "Pozières ' Flers Courcelette, "Morval, ' Thiepval ' "Le Transloy Ancre Heights' ' Ancre, 1916, 18 " "**Arras, 1917,**" "Scarpe, 1917 ' "Messines 1917," ' Pilckem "Passchendaele,' "Cambrai, 1917 '18 " St Quentin ' Avre "**Amiens,**" "Bapaume, 1918 " "**Hindenburg Line,**" Epéhy St Quentin Canal," "Selle Sambre ' "France and Flanders 1914–18 ' "**Struma,**" Doiran, 1918 ' Macedonia, 1915–18 ' Gaza, "**Jerusalem,**" Tell 'Asur ' ' Palestine, 1917–18 ' ' Aden ' Tigris, 1916 ' Kut al Amara 1917 ' "**Baghdad,**" Mesopotamia 1915–18 '

THE KING'S OWN ROYAL REGIMENT (LANCASTER)

THE GREAT WAR—16 Battalions

' Le Cateau Retreat from Mons "**Marne, 1914,**" Aisne, 1914 " ' Armentières 1914 "**Ypres, 1915, '17,**" "Gravenstafel " "St Julien," "Frezenberg, ' Bellewaarde,' "Festubert 1915 Loos," "**Somme, 1916, '18,**" ' Albert 1916, 18 ' "Bazentin Delville Wood," ' Pozières' Guillemont " ' Ginchy " "Flers Courcelette,' "Morval," "Le Transloy ' Ancre Heights, Ancre, 1916 ' "**Arras, 1917, '18,**" "Scarpe, 1917, '18,' ' Arleux " "**Messines, 1917,**" "Pilckem ' ' Menin Road Polygon Wood " "Broodseinde " "Poelcappelle ' "Passchendaele " Cambrai 1917 '18 ' St Quentin " "**Lys,**" Estaires Hazebrouck,' Béthune ' 'Bapaume 1918 Drocourt Quéant' "Hindenburg Line "Canal du Nord, 'Selle ' "Valenciennes," "Sambre,' "**France and Flanders, 1914–18** " Struma ' "Doiran 1917 '18 "**Macedonia, 1915–18** " Suvla " Sari Bair, "**Gallipoli, 1915** " "Egypt 1916 Tigris 1916," ' Kut al Amara 1917 ' Baghdad "**Mesopotamia, 1916–18** "

THE NORTHUMBERLAND FUSILIERS

THE GREAT WAR—52 Battalions

"**Mons**," Le Cateau, Retreat from Mons,' "**Marne, 1914**," "Aisne 1914 '18" La Bassée 1914,' "Messines 1914, '17, '18 Armentières 1914 "**Ypres, 1914, '15, '17, '18**," Nonne Bosschen' "Gravenstafel "**St Julien**," "Frezenberg Bellewaarde' Loos, "**Somme, 1916, '18**," "Albert 1916 '18" 'Bazentin" Delville Wood,' Pozières 'Flers Courcelette "Morval, Thiepval 'Le Transloy Ancre Heights,' Ancre 1916 'Arras 1917, 18 ' "**Scarpe, 1917, '18**," 'Arleux' Pilckem 'Langemarck, 1917 ' "Menin Road Polygon Wood," "Broodseinde 'Passchendaele' Cambrai 1917, 18 ' 'St Quentin" "Bapaume 1918' "Rosières" 'Lys,' "Estaires' "Hazebrouck" "Bailleul Kemmel Béthune, Scherpenberg,' "Drocourt Quéant, Hindenburg Line' "Épéhy' "Canal du Nord,' St Quentin Canal' 'Beaurevoir "Courtrai' "**Selle**," "Valenciennes," "Sambre France and Flanders 1914–18 "**Piave**,"' Vittorio Veneto' Italy 1917–18 ' "**Struma**," Macedonia 1915–18." "**Suvla**," "Landing at Suvla "Scimitar Hill" Gallipoli 1915' "Egypt 1916–17

THE ROYAL WARWICKSHIRE REGIMENT

THE GREAT WAR—30 Battalions

"**Le Cateau**," Retreat from Mons, "**Marne, 1914**," Aisne, 1914 18 "Armentières 1914," "**Ypres, 1914, '15, '17**," 'Langemarck 1914 '17" Gheluvelt' 'Neuve Chapelle "St Julien,' "Frezenberg,' Bellewaarde, Aubers' 'Festubert, 1915" Loos" "**Somme, 1916, '18**," 'Albert, 1916 '18" "Bazentin' Delville Wood,' Pozières," 'Guillemont Flers Courcelette,' "Morval,' 'Le Transloy ' Ancre Heights Ancre, 1916" "**Arras, 1917, '18**," "Vimy 1917' "Scarpe 1917 '18 ' Arleux" "Oppy' Bullecourt' Messines, 1917 18, Pilckem, Menin Road" 'Polygon Wood" 'Broodseinde, "Poelcappelle" Passchendaele" "Cambrai, 1917, '18 '"St. Quentin" 'Bapaume 1918," "Rosières "**Lys**," 'Estaires "Hazebrouck Bailleul,' "Kemmel" "Béthune, Drocourt Quéant" "**Hindenburg Line**," 'Épéhy 'Canal du Nord' 'Beaurevoir "Selle, "Valenciennes' Sambre" 'France and Flanders, 1914–18 ' "**Piave**," 'Vittorio Veneto, Italy, 1917–18" "Suvla,' "**Sari Bair**," Gallipoli, 1915– 16" 'Tigris 1916 "Kut al Amara 1917, "**Baghdad**," 'Mesopotamia 1916–18 "Baku ' "Persia 1918

THE ROYAL FUSILIERS (CITY OF LONDON REGIMENT)

THE GREAT WAR—47 Battalions

" **Mons,**" Le Cateau   Retreat from Mons   " **Marne, 1914,**" "Aisne 1914," "La Bassée, 1914,'   Messines, 1914, '17 " "Armentières 1914 " " **Ypres, 1914, '15, '17, '18,**" ' Nonne Bosschen " "Gravenstafel " 'St Julien ' "Frezenberg,   Belle waarde "   Hooge, 1915   'Loos," " **Somme, 1916, '18,**" Albert, 1916, 18,' " Bazentin, ' "Delville Wood   " Pozières Flers Courcelette '   'Thiepval   'Le Transloy   Ancre Heights, '   'Ancre, 1916 18   " **Arras, 1917, '18,**"   Vimy, 1917 ' "Scarpe, 1917,' 'Arleux   Pilckem,' " Langemarck 1917 ' ' Menin   Road '   "Polygon   Wood "   "Broodseinde,'   'Poel cappelle   'Passchendaele," " **Cambrai, 1917, '18,**"   ' St Quentin   Bapaume   1918   'Rosières,   Avre,   ' Villers Bretonneux   "Lys "   Estaires   "Hazebrouck,   ' Béthune " "Amiens "   Drocourt Quéant   " **Hindenburg   Line,**" Havrincourt   ' Épéhy,'   " Canal du Nord,"   " St   Quentin Canal," "Beaurevoir," "Courtrai," " Selle "   'Sambre '   'France and Flanders 1914–18   'Italy, 1917–18 "   " **Struma,**"   Mace donia, 1915–18. '   ' Helles, '   " **Landing at Helles,**" ' Krithia "Suvla ' ' Scimitar Hill '   Gallipoli, 1915–16." "Egypt   1916 Megiddo,   'Nablus ' " **Palestine, 1918** "   ' Troitsa '   'Arch angel 1919.   " Kilimanjaro '   " Behobeho   ' Nyangao   " E Africa 1915–17

THE KING'S REGIMENT (LIVERPOOL)

THE GREAT WAR—45 Battalions

Mons,   " **Retreat from Mons,**" " **Marne, 1914,**" " **Aisne, 1914,**" " **Ypres, 1914, '15, '17,**"   Langemarck 1914, 17 ' "Gheluvelt ' "Nonne Bosschen '   Neuve Chapelle,   "Graven stafel "   'St Julien,'   'Frezenberg   "Bellewaarde '   Aubers ' " **Festubert, 1915,**" " **Loos,**" " **Somme, 1916, '18,**" ' Albert, 1916   18 '   "Bazentin '   Delville   Wood '   "Guillemont ' "Ginchy '   Flers Courcelette,   "Morval '   Le Transloy, Ancre 1916,'   Bapaume 1917,   18,' " **Arras, 1917, '18,**" " **Scarpe, 1917, '18,**" "Arleux,'   'Pilckem,' "Menin Road, Polygon Wood   Poelcappelle '   Passchendaele ' " **Cambrai, 1917, '18,**" "St   Quentin '   Rosières," "Avre,' "Lys " "Estaires '   Messines, 1918 "   Bailleul, "Kemmel," ' Béthune ' Scherpenberg,'   "Drocourt Quéant "   'Hindenburg   Line Épéhy "   'Canal du Nord "   St. Quentin Canal "   ' Selle ' ' Sambre   ' France and Flanders 1914–18   Doiran   1917 ' Macedonia 1915–18   "N W Frontier India 1915 '   "Archangel 1918–19 '

THE NORFOLK REGIMENT

THE GREAT WAR—20 Battalions

" **Mons,**" " **Le Cateau,**" Retreat from Mons " **Marne, 1914,**" " Aisne 1914,' " La Bassée, 1914 ' " **Ypres, 1914, '15, '17, '18,**" Gravenstafel ' St Julien, Frezenberg, ' Belle waarde, ' Loos, ' " **Somme, 1916, '18,**" " Albert, 1916, '18 ' ' Delville Wood," Pozières, ' Guillemont Flers Courcelette Morval, ' Thiepval ' Le Transloy ' Ancre Heights Ancre 1916 18 " ' Arras, 1917, Vimy 1917 " Scarpe, 1917 Arleux ' " Oppy ' Pilckem " Langemarck 1917 ' ' Polygon Wood," Broodseinde,' " Poelcappelle ' ' Passchendaele " Cambrai, 1917, 18 " St Quentin, ' ' Bapaume 1918," " Lys Bailleul ' ' Kemmel Scherpenberg " " Amiens ' " **Hindenburg Line,**" ' Épéhy, Canal du Nord ' St Quentin Canal, Beaurevoir ' Selle ' Sambre " ' France and Flanders 1914– 18 ' ' Italy, 1917–18 ' Suvla, " **Landing at Suvla,**" Scimitar Hill " Gallipoli 1915 ' ' Egypt 1915–17 ' " **Gaza,**" El Mughar ' Nebi Samwil, Jerusalem, Jaffa, " Tell Asur, " Megiddo ' " Sharon, ' Palestine 1917–18 " " **Shaiba,**" " **Kut al Amara, 1915, '17,**" Ctesiphon ' " Defence of Kut al Amara ' Mesopotamia 1914–18

THE LINCOLNSHIRE REGIMENT

THE GREAT WAR—19 Battalions

" **Mons,**" Le Cateau, Retreat from Mons ' " **Marne, 1914,**" " Aisne, 1914, '18 La Bassée 1914 " " **Messines, 1914, '17, '18,**" Armentières 1914 ' " **Ypres, 1914, '15, '17,**" Nonne Bosschen ' " **Neuve Chapelle,**" Gravenstafel ' St Julien " Frezenberg " Bellewaarde," " Aubers ' " **Loos,**" " **Somme, 1916, '18,**" ' Albert 1916 '18 " Bazentin, Delville Wood " " Pozières,' ' Flers Courcelette ' Morval ' " Thiepval ' ' Ancre 1916, 18 ' Arras 1917 '18 " Scarpe, 1917, 18 Arleux ' Pilckem, " Langemarck 1917 " ' Menin Road Polygon Wood " Broodseinde," " Poelcappelle " " Passchen daele ' " Cambrai 1917, 18, ' " St. Quentin " " Bapaume 1918 ' " **Lys,**" ' Estaires,' ' Bailleul " Kemmel, Amiens, Dro court Quéant " **Hindenburg Line,**" " Épéhy, ' Canal du Nord ' " St. Quentin Canal ' " Beaurevoir ' Selle, Sambre " ' France and Flanders, 1914–18. " **Suvla,**" Landing at Suvla Scimitar Hill ' " Gallipoli 1915 ' Egypt 1916 "

THE DEVONSHIRE REGIMENT

THE GREAT WAR—25 Battalions

Aisne 1914, 18 "**La Bassée, 1914,**" Armentières, 1914 Neuve Chapelle ' Hill 60," "**Ypres, 1915, '17,**" "Graven stafel 'St Julien," Frezenberg, "Aubers,' "**Loos,**" "**Somme, 1916, '18,**" Albert 1916, Bazentin Delville Wood, "Guillemont," Flers Courcelette "Morval, 'Arras, 1917" Vimy 1917,' Scarpe 1917 "Bullecourt "Pilckem" Langemarck, 1917 ' Polygon Wood "Broodseinde" Poel cappelle 'Passchendaele," "Rosières, Villers Bretonneux ' "Lys ' Hazebrouck" "**Bois des Buttes,**" "Marne, 1918 Tardenois " "Bapaume 1918 ' "**Hindenburg Line,**" 'Havrin court,' Épéhy ' 'Canal du Nord ' "Beaurevoir" Cambrai, 1918 ' Selle,' Sambre 'France and Flanders 1914–18 ' 'Piave, "**Vittorio Veneto,**" "Italy 1917–18 "**Doiran, 1917, '18,**" Macedonia 1915–18 "Egypt, 1916 17 'Gaza,' "Nebi Samwil 'Jerusalem Tell Asur," "**Palestine, 1917–18.**" 'Tigris 1916 " "Kut al Amara 1917 "**Mesopotamia, 1916–18 '**

THE SUFFOLK REGIMENT

THE GREAT WAR—22 Battalions

Mons, "**Le Cateau,**" Retreat from Mons Marne 1914 Aisne, 1914,' La Bassée, 1914 " 'Givenchy 1914 " "**Neuve Chapelle,**" "**Ypres, 1915, '17, '18,**" 'Gravenstafel ' "St. Julien "' Frezenberg,' 'Bellewaarde," "Aubers,' 'Hooge 1915 " "Loos, "**Somme, 1916, '18,**" "Albert, 1916 '18 ' "Bazentin Delville Wood 'Pozières,' Flers Courcelette "Morval Thiepval, "Le Transloy ' "Ancre Heights ' "Ancre, 1916, 18 "**Arras, 1917, '18,**" "Scarpe 1917 18 ' "Arleux,' ' Pilckem Langemarck, 1917 Menin Road 'Polygon Wood,' "Poel cappelle "Passchendaele "**Cambrai, 1917, '18,**" "St. Quentin Bapaume, 1918, Lys "Estaires,' Messines, 1918 " "Hazebrouck ' "Bailleul,' Kemmel ' "Béthune " "Scherpen berg,' "Amiens "**Hindenburg Line,**" "Épéhy, Canal du Nord, 'Courtrai, Selle,' "Valenciennes Sambre, "France and Flanders 1914–18.' "Struma " Doiran, 1918, "**Macedonia, 1915–18.**" 'Suvla,' "**Landing at Suvla,**" 'Scimitar Hill " "Gallipoli 1915 ' "Egypt 1915–17 ' "**Gaza,**" "El Mughar 'Nebi Samwil ' Jerusalem ' Jaffa Tell 'Asur "Megiddo Sharon ' "Palestine 1917–18

THE SOMERSET LIGHT INFANTRY (PRINCE ALBERT'S)

— — —

THE GREAT WAR—16 Battalions

Le Cateau Retreat from Mons **"Marne, 1914, '18,"** **"Aisne, 1914,"** Armentières 1914," **"Ypres, 1915, '17, '18,"** St Julien,' Frezenberg,' 'Bellewaarde,' "Hooge 1915, Loos '"Mount Sorrel **"Somme, 1916, '18,"** **"Albert, 1916, '18,"** Delville Wood 'Guillemont,' "Flers Courcelette,' 'Morval, "Le Transloy, Ancre 1916 18' **"Arras, 1917, '18,"** Vimy 1917 "Scarpe, 1917 18, Arleux 'Langemarck 1917,' 'Menin Road' 'Polygon Wood" 'Broodseinde, "Poelcappelle "Passchendaele,' **"Cambrai, 1917, '18,"** "St Quentin," 'Bapaume, 1918' "Rosières" Avre,' 'Lys'' Hazebrouck," Béthune' 'Soissonnais Ourcq' 'Drocourt Quéant, **"Hindenburg Line,"** 'Havrincourt' Épéhy,' "Canal du Nord," "Courtrai "Selle "Valenciennes,' "Sambre "France and Flanders, 1914 18 "Gaza," El Mughar' 'Nebi Samwil "Jerusalem,' 'Megiddo "Sharon **"Palestine, 1917–18."** **"Tigris, 1916,"** "Sharqat "Mesopotamia 1916-18' 'N W Frontier India 1915'

THE WEST YORKSHIRE REGIMENT (THE PRINCE OF WALES'S OWN)

— — —

THE GREAT WAR—31 Battalions

Aisne 1914, 18 **"Armentières, 1914,"** **"Neuve Chapelle,"** Aubers 'Hooge, 1915 "Loos' **"Somme, 1916, '18,"** Albert, 1916, 18,"' Bazentin 'Pozières "Flers Courcelette Morval' "Thiepval' 'Le Transloy 'Ancre Heights Ancre 1916 "Arras 1917 '18,' "Scarpe 1917 '18,' "Bullecourt' Hill 70 "Messines, 1917 18,' **"Ypres, 1917, '18,"** 'Pilckem "'Langemarck 1917,'' Menin Road," 'Polygon Wood, Poelcappelle' "Passchendaele **"Cambrai, 1917, '18,"** St Quentin,' Rosières' **"Villers Bretonneux,"** **"Lys,"** Hazebrouck" Bailleul' Kemmel,' Marne 1918 **"Tardenois,"** Amiens "Bapaume, 1918' Drocourt Quéant, 'Hindenburg Line, 'Havrincourt' Épéhy, "Canal du Nord 'Selle" "Valenciennes,' 'Sambre" France and Flanders 1914–18 **"Piave,"** Vittorio Veneto "Italy, 1917–18' **"Suvla,"** Landing at Suvla' 'Scimitar Hill 'Gallipoli 1915 'Egypt 1915–16"

  C

THE EAST YORKSHIRE REGIMENT

THE GREAT WAR—21 Battalions

"**Aisne, 1914, '18,**" "**Armentières, 1914,**" "**Ypres, 1915, '17, '18,**" ' Gravenstafel " " St Julien ' Frezenberg,' ' Belle waarde " Hooge 1915 "**Loos,**" "**Somme, 1916, '18,**" ' Albert, 1916 '18, " Bazentin ' Delville Wood ' Pozières Flers Courcelette,' Morval," Thiepval " Ancre Heights Ancre 1916,' "**Arras, 1917, '18,**" ' Scarpe 1917 '18 Arleux,' ' Oppy, " Messines 1917 18 ' Pilckem Lange marck 1917,' " Menin Road ' Polygon Wood Brood seinde " Poelcappelle ' " Passchendaele " "**Cambrai, 1917, '18,**" St Quentin " Bapaume, 1918 Rosières " Lys ' ' Estaires,' ' Hazebrouck ' " Kemmel, " Scherpenberg Amiens ' Hindenburg Line Épéhy " Canal du Nord St Quentin Canal ' "**Selle,**" Sambre,' France and Flanders 1914–18.' " Struma "**Doiran, 1917,**" Macedonia 1915 18 ' Suvla ' Landing at Suvla ' Scimitar Hill ' "**Gallipoli, 1915** " Egypt 1915–16

THE BEDFORDSHIRE AND HERTFORDSHIRE REGIMENT

THE GREAT WAR— 18 Battalions

"**Mons,**" Le Cateau Retreat from Mons "**Marne, 1914,**" Aisne 1914 La Bassée 1914 "**Ypres, 1914, '15, '17,**" ' Langemarck 1914 17,' ' Gheluvelt ' " Nonne Bosschen Neuve Chapelle ' Hill 60,' " St Julien,' " Frezenberg Bellewaarde,' " Aubers ' " Festubert, 1915, ' "**Loos,**" "**Somme, 1916, '18,**" ' Albert 1916 18 ' " Bazentin " Delville Wood ' ' Pozières, Guillemont, Flers Courcelette ' " Morval Thiepval, Le Transloy," Ancre Heights ' ' Ancre, 1916, 18 "**Arras, 1917, '18,**" ' Vimy 1917,' " Scarpe, 1917 ' " Arleux Oppy,' " Messines 1917 ' ' Pilckem,' " Polygon Wood, Broodseinde ' " Poelcappelle " Passchendaele ' "**Cambrai, 1917, '18,**" St Quentin Bapaume 1918 Rosières ' " Avre ' Villers Bretonneux " Lys,' Hazebrouck Scherpenberg ' Amiens ' " Drocourt Quéant " Hindenburg Line, " Épéhy, ' Canal du Nord, St Quentin Canal " ' Selle " **Sambre,**" " France and Flanders 1914–18 " ' Italy, 1917–18 "**Suvla,**" ' Landing at Suvla ' Scimitar Hill ' ' Gallipoli 1915 ' Egypt 1915 17 ' "**Gaza,**" " El Mughar Nebi Samwil, Jerusalem, ' Jaffa Tell Asur " Megiddo Sharon " Palestine 1917–18 '

THE LEICESTERSHIRE REGIMENT

THE GREAT WAR—19 Battalions

"**Aisne, 1914, '18,**" La Bassée 1914 Armentières 1914 Festubert 1914 15,' "**Neuve Chapelle,**" ' Aubers ' " Hooge, 1915 "**Somme, 1916, '18,**" Bazentin, Flers Courcelette ' Morval " Le Transloy, "**Ypres, 1917,**" ' Polygon Wood "**Cambrai, 1917, '18,**" ' St Quentin,' "**Lys,**" " Bailleul Kemmel Scherpenberg, Albert, 1918 " Bapaume, 1918 Hindenburg Line 'Épéhy "**St Quentin Canal,**" Beaurevoir ' " Selle ' Sambre "**France and Flanders, 1914-18 **" Megiddo Sharon, Damascus " "**Palestine, 1918 **" Tigris 1916 Kut al Amara 1917 ' Baghdad " "**Mesopotamia, 1915-18 **"

THE ROYAL IRISH REGIMENT

THE GREAT WAR—9 Battalions

"**Mons,**" "**Le Cateau,**" Retreat from Mons "**Marne, 1914,**" " Aisne 1914 ' "La Bassée 1914, ' "**Ypres, 1915, '17, '18,**" Gravenstafel, ' St Julien ' Frezenberg, ' Belle waarde, "**Somme, 1916, '18,**" " Albert, 1916 18 ' Bazentin,' ' Delville Wood " Guillemont " ' Ginchy, "**Messines, 1917,**" Pilckem ' Langemarck 1917 ' St Quentin ' " Rosières " Arras 1918, " Drocourt Quéant, "**Hindenburg Line,**" " Canal du Nord,' St. Quentin Canal Beaurevoir " " Cambrai 1918 ' ' Courtrai, " France and Flanders, 1914–18 "**Struma,**" ' Macedonia 1915–17." "**Suvla,**" " Landing at Suvla " " Gallipoli, 1915.' "**Gaza,**" Jerusalem Tell Asur ' " Megiddo ' " Nablus ' ' Palestine 1917–18

THE GREEN HOWARDS (ALEXANDRA, PRINCESS OF WALES'S OWN YORKSHIRE REGIMENT)

THE GREAT WAR—24 Battalions

"**Ypres, 1914, '15, '17,**" Langemarck, 1914 17 Gheluvelt Neuve Chapelle St Julien," ' Frezenberg Bellewaarde, Aubers ' Festubert, 1915 "**Loos,**" "**Somme, 1916, '18,**" ' Albert, 1916 Bazentin, Pozières Flers Courcelette, Morval,' ' Thiepval Le Transloy, Ancre Heights, ' Ancre 1916, "**Arras, 1917, '18,**" "Scarpe, 1917, '18 " "**Messines, 1917, '18,**" ' Pilckem ' Menin Road " ' Polygon Wood ' Broodseinde,' Poelcappelle ' "Passchendaele ' Cambrai 1917, 18 ' "St Quentin ' ' Bapaume 1918 ' "Rosières ' "Lys ' "Estaires,' "Hazebrouck " "Kemmel Scherpenberg " ' Aisne 1918 " Drocourt Quéant " Hindenburg Line Canal du Nord "Beaurevoir ' Selle ' "**Valenciennes,**" "**Sambre,**" "**France and Flanders, 1914–18 **" "Piave "**Vittorio Veneto,**" Italy 1917–18. ' "**Suvla,**" Landing at Suvla ' Scimitar Hill " Gallipoli 1915 ' Egypt 1916 Archangel 1918 "

THE LANCASHIRE FUSILIERS

THE GREAT WAR—30 Battalions

Le Cateau "**Retreat from Mons,**" Marne, 1914, "**Aisne, 1914, '18,**" Armentières 1914,' "**Ypres, 1915, '17, '18,**" ' St Julien, Bellewaarde "**Somme, 1916, '18,**" ' Albert, 1916 '18 ' ' Bazentin ' Delville Wood ' Pozières Ginchy " Flers Courcelette ' Morval,' Thiepval ' "Le Transloy Ancre Heights ' Ancre, 1916 18 "**Arras, 1917, '18,**" Scarpe 1917 18, "Arleux Messines 1917 Pilckem Langemarck 1917 Menin Road," ' Polygon Wood Broodseinde ' Poelcappelle, "**Passchendaele,**" "**Cambrai, 1917, '18,**" St Quentin " Bapaume, 1918,' Rosières " "Lys, "Estaires ' ' Hazebrouck ' "Bailleul Kemmel Béthune,' Scherpenberg,' Amiens "Drocourt Quéant, "**Hindenburg Line,**" "Épéhy, ' Canal du Nord ' " St. Quentin Canal, ' "Courtrai ' Selle " "Sambre " ' France and Flanders, 1914–18 "Doiran 1917, ' "**Macedonia, 1915–18.**" ' Helles " "**Landing at Helles,**" "Krithia ' "Suvla ' Landing at Suvla Scimitar Hill 'Gallipoli 1915 Rumani "Egypt 1915 17

THE ROYAL SCOTS FUSILIERS

THE GREAT WAR—18 Battalions

"**Mons,**" Le Cateau Retreat from Mons "**Marne, 1914,**" Aisne 1914 ' ' La Bassée, 1914, ' "**Ypres, 1914, '17, '18,**" Langemarck 1914 ' Gheluvelt ' Nonne Bosschen ' Neuve Chapelle," Aubers ' Festubert 1915 " ' Loos " "**Somme, 1916, '18,**" 'Albert, 1916 18," " Bazentin Delville Wood ' Pozières, Flers Courcelette,' Le Transloy Ancre Heights Ancre 1916, ' "**Arras, 1917, '18,**" ' Scarpe 1917, '18 ' Arleux Messines 1917, Pilckem,' ' Menin Road ' "Polygon Wood St Quentin ' ' Bapaume, 1918 Rosières "**Lys,**" "Estaires Hazebrouck " Bailleul, ' Béthune, " Scherpenberg Drocourt Quéant "**Hindenburg Line,**" Canal du Nord Courtrai Selle France and Flanders 1914 18. "**Doiran, 1917, '18,**" Macedonia, 1916–18 ' " Helles, ' "**Gallipoli, 1915 16 "** Rumani ' "Egypt 1916–17 Gaza ' El Mughar ' "Nebi Samwil, " Jerusalem " Jaffa Tell Asur " **Palestine, 1917–18 "**

THE CHESHIRE REGIMENT

THE GREAT WAR— 38 Battalions

"**Mons,**" Le Cateau, Retreat from Mons, Marne 1914 18, ' ' Aisne 1914, '18 ' La Bassée, 1914,' Armentières, 1914 "**Ypres, 1914, '15, '17, '18,**" ' Nonne Bosschen " ' Gravenstafel ' St Julien ' Frezenberg "Bellewaarde Loos," "**Somme, 1916, '18,**" Albert 1916, 18 ' ' Bazentin Delville Wood," ' Pozières ' Guillemont ' Flers Courcelette Morval Thiepval, ' Le Transloy "Ancre Heights " 'Ancre, 1916 ' "**Arras, 1917, '18,**" " Vimy, 1917," ' Scarpe 1917 '18, ' Oppy "**Messines, 1917, '18,**" ' Pilckem " ' Langemarck 1917 ' Menin Road ' Polygon Wood, " Broodseinde," " Poel cappelle ' " Passchendaele, ' Cambrai, 1917 18 ' " St Quentin "**Bapaume, 1918,**" Rosières, "Lys ' ' Estaires, Hazebrouck Bailleul, ' ' Kemmel," ' Scherpenberg " " Soissonnais Ourcq Hindenburg Line ' ' Canal du Nord Courtrai ' ' Selle Valenciennes, ' " Sambre ' France and Flanders, 1914–18 Italy, 1917–18 ' Struma "**Doiran, 1917, '18,**" " Macedonia 1915–18. ' "**Suvla,**" " Sari Bair ' ' Landing at Suvla, ' Scimitar Hill " Gallipoli 1915.' "Egypt, 1915–17 ' "**Gaza,**" " El Mughar, " Jerusalem,' Jericho," " Tell Asur " Palestine, 1917–18 Tigris 1916, "**Kut al Amara, 1917,**" Baghdad ' Mesopotamia 1916–18 '

THE ROYAL WELCH FUSILIERS

THE GREAT WAR—42 Battalions

Mons   Le Cateau   Retreat from Mons   "**Marne, 1914,**" Aisne 1914 '18," "La Bassée 1914, 'Messines 1914 17 '18, Armentières 1914   "**Ypres, 1914, '17, '18,**" "Langemarck, 1914 '17, "Gheluvelt 'Givenchy 1914 'Neuve Chapelle" 'Aubers 'Festubert, 1915 '"Loos,' "**Somme, 1916, '18,**" Albert 1916, 18, '"Bazentin "Delville Wood' "Pozières Guillemont" 'Flers Courcelette, 'Morval '"Le Transloy Ancre Heights "Ancre 1916, '18 "Arras 1917 "Scarpe, 1917, Arleux, Bullecourt, ''Pilckem' 'Menin Road" 'Polygon Wood   Broodseinde, "Poelcappelle' "Passchendaele" "Cambrai, 1917 '18" 'St. Quentin" "Bapaume 1918' "Lys, Bailleul' "Kemmel, 'Scherpenberg "**Hindenburg Line,**" Havrincourt 'Épéhy' St Quentin Canal 'Beaurevoir" "Selle Valenciennes, "Sambre, France and Flanders 1914–18 Piave, "**Vittorio Veneto,**" "Italy 1917–18' "**Doiran, 1917, '18,**" "Macedonia 1915–18' Suvla," 'Sari Bair, "Landing at Suvla Scimitar Hill,' "**Gallipoli, 1915–16.**" 'Rumani" "**Egypt, 1915–17**" "**Gaza,**" 'El Mughar' Jerusalem Jericho "Tell Asur, "Megiddo 'Nablus 'Palestine, 1917–18 'Tigris, 1916,' Kut al Amara 1917" "**Baghdad,**" 'Mesopotamia 1916–18'

THE SOUTH WALES BORDERERS

THE GREAT WAR—18 Battalions

"**Mons,**" Retreat from Mons, "**Marne, 1914,**" Aisne, 1914 '18" "**Ypres, 1914, '17, '18,**" 'Langemarck, 1914 '17" "**Gheluvelt,**" "Nonne Bosschen, 'Givenchy 1914," "Aubers Loos,' "**Somme, 1916, '18,**"' Albert 1916 '18" Bazentin Pozières,' 'Flers Courcelette, Morval Ancre Heights Ancre, 1916' "Arras 1917, '18 "Scarpe 1917' Messines, 1917 '18,' Pilckem 'Menin Road' 'Polygon Wood" 'Broodseinde, "Poelcappelle" 'Passchendaele "**Cambrai, 1917, '18,**" "St. Quentin, '"Bapaume 1918, '"Lys, Estaires' "Hazebrouck' 'Bailleul 'Kemmel' 'Béthune' Scherpenberg' "Drocourt Quéant Hindenburg Line" "Havrincourt' "Épéhy" "St Quentin Canal" "Beaurevoir 'Courtrai Selle' Valenciennes" 'Sambre "France and Flanders, 1914–18 "**Doiran, 1917, '18,**" Macedonia 1915–18" 'Helles "**Landing at Helles,**" Krithia,' "Suvla,' Sari Bair' 'Scimitar Hill,' Gallipoli, 1915–16' Egypt 1916' "Tigris 1916' Kut al Amara, 1917' "**Baghdad,**" Mesopotamia 1916–18 "**Tsingtao**"

THE KING'S OWN SCOTTISH BORDERERS

- —

THE GREAT WAR—12 Battalions

" **Mons,** " Le Cateau, Retreat from Mons Marne, 1914,
18, " **Aisne, 1914,** " ' La Bassée 1914,' " Messines, 1914 "
" **Ypres, 1914, '15, '17, '18,** " " Nonne Bosschen " " Hill 60
Gravenstafel ' " St. Julien, Frezenberg," " Bellewaarde
" **Loos,** " " **Somme, 1916, '18,** " Albert 1916 18 ' Bazentin
Delville Wood ' " Pozières ' Guillemont ' Flers Courcelette,
Morval, Le Transloy ' Ancre Heights, " **Arras, 1917,
'18,** " ' Vimy 1917 " ' Scarpe, 1917, 18," Arleux " Pilckem '
Langemarck, 1917 Menin Road ' " Polygon Wood " Brood
scinde, Poelcappelle, " Passchendaele, ' ' Cambrai 1917 18 '
St Quentin,' " Lys ' Estaires ' " Hazebrouck Kemmel
" **Soissonnais-Ourcq,** " ' Bapaume, 1918 " " Drocourt Quéant
" **Hindenburg Line,** " Épéhy ' ' Canal du Nord " " Courtrai
Selle " ' Sambre " France and Flanders, 1914–18 " Italy,
1917 18 " Helles, Landing at Helles,' ' Krithia, Suvla '
Scimitar Hill ' " **Gallipoli, 1915-16.** " Rumani, Egypt,
1916.' " **Gaza,** " " El Mughar ' " Nebi Samwil " Jaffa "
Palestine 1917-18

THE CAMERONIANS (SCOTTISH RIFLES)

- -

THE GREAT WAR—27 Battalions

" **Mons,** " Le Cateau, Retreat from Mons, " **Marne, 1914,
'18,** " " Aisne 1914 ' ' La Bassée 1914 ' ' Messines, 1914 '
" Armentières, 1914,' " **Neuve Chapelle,** " Aubers " " **Loos,** "
" **Somme, 1916, '18,** " " Albert, 1916 ' Bazentin ' Pozières
Flers Courcelette " ' Le Transloy Ancre Heights, ' " Arras,
1917 '18 " Scarpe 1917, '18 ' Arleux, " **Ypres, 1917, '18,** "
' Pilckem, ' Langemarck 1917," ' Menin Road ' Polygon
Wood ' " Passchendaele,' St Quentin ' Rosières " Avre "
' Lys Hazebrouck ' ' Bailleul," " Kemmel, ' " Scherpenberg
Soissonnais Ourcq ' Drocourt Quéant " **Hindenburg Line,** "
Épéhy," " Canal du Nord ' ' St. Quentin Canal " " Cambrai
1918 " ' Courtrai ' " Selle," Sambre,' " France and Flanders,
1914–18 " Doiran 1917 18,' " **Macedonia, 1915–18** "
" **Gallipoli, 1915** " ' Rumani,' Egypt, 1916 17 ' Gaza
El Mughar ' " Nebi Samwil " " Jaffa " " **Palestine, 1917–18** "

THE ROYAL INNISKILLING FUSILIERS

THE GREAT WAR - 12 Battalions

"**Le Cateau,**" Retreat from Mons   Marne, 1914,   Aisne, 1914   Messines 1914, 17 " ' Armentières 1914,' ' Aubers " " Festubert, 1915   "**Somme, 1916, '18,**" ' Albert 1916   Bazentin,' " Guillemont " Ginchy ' Ancre, 1916, 'Arras, 1917 ' " Scarpe, 1917   "**Ypres, 1917, '18,**" " Pilckem ' ' Langemarck 1917 '   Polygon Wood   Broodseinde   Poelcappelle, ' Cambrai, 1917   18 '   "**St Quentin,**" Rosières ' "**Hindenburg Line,**" Beaurevoir '   Courtrai ' Selle   Sambre ' "**France and Flanders, 1914-18** " Kostuino ' " Struma, "**Macedonia, 1915-17.**" ' Helles "**Landing at Helles,**" Krithia ' " Suvla, ' Landing at Suvla   " Scimitar Hill, ' "**Gallipoli, 1915-16** " Egypt 1916 " " Gaza   ' Jerusalem '   Tell Asur ' "**Palestine, 1917-18** "

THE GLOUCESTERSHIRE REGIMENT

THE GREAT WAR—24 Battalions

"**Mons,**"   Retreat from Mons,   Marne 1914   Aisne, 1914 '18 " "**Ypres, 1914, '15, '17,**"   Langemarck, 1914 '17 ' ' Gheluvelt ' Nonne Bosschen   " Givenchy 1914,' ' Graven stafel ' St Julien ' ' Frezenberg ' Bellewaarde,'   Aubers "**Loos,**" "**Somme, 1916, '18,**" ' Albert 1916 '18 "   Bazentin Delville Wood " " Pozières,' ' Guillemont,' " Flers Courcelette Morval, " Ancre Heights,' Ancre 1916,   Arras 1917 18 Vimy 1917, ' " Scarpe 1917   " Messines 1917 '18, ' ' Pilckem Menin Road,   Polygon Wood   " Broodseinde   ' Poelcappelle Passchendaele ' Cambrai, 1917   18 " ' St Quentin, ' Bapaume, 1918,' " Rosières, ' Avre " "**Lys,**"   Estaires, " Hazebrouck ' " Bailleul,   " Kemmel,'   Béthune "   ' Drocourt Quéant, Hindenburg Line ' " Épéhy, " Canal du Nord ' ' St Quentin Canal ' ' Beaurevoir   "**Selle,**" " Valenciennes   " Sambre ' France and Flanders 1914-18 "   Piave " "**Vittorio Veneto,**" Italy, 1917-18 "   ' Struma,' "**Doiran, 1917,**" " Macedonia 1915-18 '   ' Suvla   "**Sari Bair,**" ' Scimitar Hill, " Gallipoli, 1915-16   Egypt 1916 ' ' Tigris 1916   " Kut al Amara 1917 ' "**Baghdad,**" " Mesopotamia 1916-18 '   Persia 1918 '

THE WORCESTERSHIRE REGIMENT

THE GREAT WAR—22 Battalions

" **Mons**," Le Cateau Retreat from Mons Marne 1914
Aisne 1914, '18, " La Bassée, 1914, " Armentières 1914
" **Ypres, 1914, '15, '17, '18**," Langemarck 1914 17
" **Gheluvelt**," ' Nonne Bosschen " **Neuve Chapelle**,"
Aubers ' ' Festubert 1915, " Loos " **Somme, 1916, '18**,"
Albert 1916 ' ' Bazentin, ' Delville Wood," " Pozières " Le
Transloy ' Ancre Heights ' Ancre 1916 ' Arras, 1917
' Scarpe, 1917,' " Arleux, ' Messines 1917, 18, ' ' Pilckem
Menin Road ' Polygon Wood " Broodseinde ' " Poelcappelle
Passchendaele, " **Cambrai, 1917, '18**," St Quentin
Bapaume, 1918 Rosières, ' ' Villers Bretonneux " **Lys**,"
' Estaires," " Hazebrouck " " Bailleul, ' Kemmel ' Scherpen
berg " Hindenburg Line " Canal du Nord ' St Quentin
Canal Beaurevoir ' " Courtrai," ' Selle ' Valenciennes,"
' Sambre " France and Flanders, 1914 18 ' Piave," " Vittorio
Veneto," " **Italy, 1917-18** " " Doiran 1917 18," " Macedonia,
1915-18 Helles ' " Landing at Helles ' Krithia ' " Suvla "
Sari Bair " Scimitar Hill," " **Gallipoli, 1915-16** " Egypt,
1916 ' ' Tigris 1916, " Kut al Amara 1917,' " **Baghdad**,"
Mesopotamia 1916-18 ' Baku ' " Persia 1918

THE EAST LANCASHIRE REGIMENT

THE GREAT WAR— 17 Battalions

Le Cateau " **Retreat from Mons**," " **Marne, 1914**,"
" **Aisne, 1914, '18**," " Armentières 1914 ' " **Neuve Chapelle**,"
" **Ypres, 1915, '17, '18**," ' St Julien,' Frezenberg," " Belle
waarde " ' Aubers, " **Somme, 1916, '18**," ' Albert 1916 18 '
' Bazentin ' ' Pozières,' ' Le Transloy Ancre Heights
Ancre 1916, 18 ' " **Arras, 1917, '18**," Vimy 1917
Scarpe 1917, 18 Arleux, " Oppy Messines 1917
Pilckem " Langemarck, 1917 Menin Road ' " Polygon
Wood,' " Broodseinde ' Poelcappelle' " Passchendaele ' St.
Quentin " Bapaume 1918 ' " Rosières, Villers Bretonneux "
' Lys " Estaires, ' Hazebrouck," ' Bailleul ' ' Kemmel
Hindenburg Line,' Canal du Nord Cambrai 1918 " ' Selle
Valenciennes " " Sambre ' " France and Flanders 1914-18
Kosturino " **Doiran, 1917, '18**," Macedonia, 1915-18
" **Helles**," Krithia ' ' Suvla ' Sari Bair," " Gallipoli, 1915
Rumani Egypt, 1915-17 Tigris 1916, " **Kut al Amara,
1917**," Baghdad " Mesopotamia 1916 17 '

THE EAST SURREY REGIMENT

THE GREAT WAR—18 Battalions

"**Mons**," Le Cateau Retreat from Mons "**Marne, 1914**," Aisne, 1914 "**La Bassée, 1914**," Armentières, 1914, "Hill 60 ' "**Ypres, 1915, '17, '18**," Gravenstafel,' St Julien ' Frezenberg ' Bellewaarde "**Loos**," "**Somme, 1916, '18**," "**Albert, 1916, '18**," Bazentin "Delville Wood "Pozières " ' Guillemont "Flers Courcelette, Morval ' Thiepval, ' 'Le Transloy' "Ancre Heights ' "Ancre, 1916 Arras 1917, 18 "Vimy 1917 " "Scarpe, 1917," "Messines, 1917," "Pilckem 'Langemarck 1917 ' "Menin Road " "Polygon Wood " Broodseinde, ' Poelcappelle, ' Passchen daele ' "**Cambrai, 1917, 18**," St Quentin,' Bapaume, 1918 ' Rosières ' Avre ' 'Lys, 'Estaires," ' Hazebrouck," ' Amiens ' "Hindenburg Line," ' Épéhy, "Canal du Nord St. Quentin Canal," 'Courtrai "**Selle**," Sambre," France and Flanders, 1914–18 "Italy 1917–18 ' Struma," "**Doiran, 1918**," "Macedonia 1915–18 ' Egypt 1915 " ' Aden " "Mesopotamia 1917–18 ' "Murman 1919 '

THE DUKE OF CORNWALL'S LIGHT INFANTRY

—

THE GREAT WAR —15 Battalions

"**Mons**," Le Cateau, Retreat from Mons "**Marne, 1914**," Aisne, 1914, La Bassée 1914 Armentières 1914 ' "**Ypres, 1915, '17**,"' Gravenstafel 'St Julien,' Frezenberg, Bellewaarde ' 'Hooge, 1915 " Mount Sorrel," "**Somme, 1916, '18**," "Delville Wood ' Guillemont," "Flers Courcelette ' 'Morval ' Le Transloy Ancre 1916 ' Bapaume 1917, 18 "**Arras, 1917**," Vimy 1917 ' "Scarpe 1917 ' ' Arleux, Langemarck 1917 Menin Road Polygon Wood "Brood seinde " Poelcappelle ' "**Passchendaele**," "**Cambrai, 1917, '18**," ' St Quentin,' Rosières, ' ' Lys, ' Estaires ' Haze brouck, ' Albert, 1918, ' "Hindenburg Line ' "Havrincourt Canal du Nord " Selle "**Sambre**," "France and Flanders, 1914–18 " 'Italy 1917–18. "Struma, "**Doiran, 1917, '18**," 'Macedonia, 1915–18 ' "**Gaza**," 'Nebi Samwil," ' Jerusalem Tell Asur " ' Megiddo Sharon Palestine 1917–18 ' "Aden

THE DUKE OF WELLINGTON'S REGIMENT
(WEST RIDING)

THE GREAT WAR—21 Battalions

" **Mons**," Le Cateau   Retreat from Mons   " **Marne, 1914, '18**," "Aisne 1914 ' "La Bassée, 1914, ' " **Ypres, 1914, '15, '17**," ' Nonne Bosschen   " **Hill 60**," Gravenstafel ' " St Julien Aubers, ' " **Somme, 1916, '18**," " Albert 1916, '18 Bazentin   Delville Wood,' Pozières   " Flers Courcelette Morval " Thiepval, 'Le Transloy ' Ancre Heights " **Arras, 1917, '18**," ' Scarpe 1917 '18 ' ' Arleux,' " Bullecourt Messines 1917 18 ' " Langemarck, 1917 ' ' Menin Road Polygon Wood   " Broodseinde, " Poelcappelle,' " Passchendaele ' " **Cambrai, 1917, '18**," " St Quentin ' " Ancre 1918 ' " **Lys**," ' Estaires ' Hazebrouck   " Bailleul ' Kemmel Béthune, " Scherpenberg," " Tardenois   Amiens, Bapaume, 1918 " " Drocourt Quéant," Hindenburg Line   " Havrincourt " Épéhy ' ' Canal du Nord, Selle, ' Valenciennes," Sambre France and Flanders 1914–18. " **Piave**," " Vittorio Veneto Italy, 1917–18 " " Suvla, ' " **Landing at Suvla**," ' Scimitar Hill " ' Gallipoli 1915 ' " Egypt 1916 '

THE BORDER REGIMENT

THE GREAT WAR—16 Battalions

" **Ypres, 1914, '15, '17, '18**," " **Langemarck, 1914, '17**," Gheluvelt ' " Neuve Chapelle," Frezenberg " Bellewaarde Aubers ' Festubert, 1915 " ' Loos, ' " **Somme, 1916, '18**," Albert 1916 '18, ' ' Bazentin ' Delville Wood,' " Pozières, Guillemont ' Flers Courcelette   Morval " Thiepval," Le Transloy " Ancre Heights   Ancre 1916 " **Arras, 1917, '18**," ' Scarpe 1917 " Bullecourt ' Messines 1917 '18," " Pilckem Polygon Wood   Broodseinde,' Poelcappelle ' Passchendaele ' " **Cambrai, 1917, '18**," St Quentin, Rosières " **Lys**," Estaires ' Hazebrouck, Bailleul ' Kemmel Scherpenberg ' " Aisne 1918, ' ' Amiens ' " Bapaume 1918 Hindenburg Line   Épéhy ' " St Quentin Canal," ' Beaurevoir, Courtrai ' ' Selle, Sambre   " **France and Flanders, 1914–18** " ' Piave ' " **Vittorio Veneto**," ' Italy, 1917–18.' " Doiran, 1917 18,' " **Macedonia, 1915–18** " " Helles   " Landing at Helles, ' " Krithia   ' Suvla, Landing at Suvla, ' Scimitar Hill ' " **Gallipoli, 1915–16** " " Egypt 1916   " N W Frontier India, 1916–17

THE ROYAL SUSSEX REGIMENT

THE GREAT WAR—23 Battalions

Mons, "**Retreat from Mons,**" "**Marne, 1914, '18,**" Aisne 1914 "**Ypres, 1914, '17, '18,**" "Gheluvelt, ' Nonne Bosschen, ' ' Givenchy, 1914," ' Aubers 'Loos ' "**Somme, 1916, '18,**" Albert, 1916, '18 Bazentin, "Delville Wood, ' " Pozières ' Flers Courcelette, Morval " Thiepval " Le Transloy, Ancre Heights ' "Ancre, 1916 18 ' ' Arras 1917, 18," " Vimy, 1917 ' Scarpe 1917 ' 'Arleux " Messines, 1917 ' "**Pilckem,**" ' Langemarck 1917 ' Menin Road " " Polygon Wood,' " Broodseinde " " Poelcappelle ' Passchendaele, ' ' Cambrai 1917 18 ' St Quentin ' ' Bapaume 1918 " " Rosières Avre, Lys ' Kemmel Scherpenberg ' Soissonnais Ourcq ' Amiens Drocourt Quéant," "**Hindenburg Line,**" Épéhy " St Quentin Canal " Beaurevoir " ' Courtrai Selle ' Sambre," " France and Flanders, 1914 18. " Piave Vittorio Veneto ' "**Italy, 1917–18**" " Suvla, ' ' Landing at Suvla " Scimitar Hill " "**Gallipoli, 1915**" " Rumani " "Egypt, 1915–17 " Gaza El Mughar ' Jerusalem ' Jericho Tell Asur "**Palestine, 1917–18**" "**N W Frontier India, 1915, 1916–17**" ' Murman 1918–19

THE HAMPSHIRE REGIMENT

THE GREAT WAR—36 Battalions

Le Cateau, "**Retreat from Mons,**" Marne, 1914 18 Aisne 1914," Armentières 1914,' "**Ypres, 1915, '17, '18,**" St. Julien,' Frezenberg " ' Bellewaarde " "**Somme, 1916, '18,**" " Albert 1916 ' Guillemont,' Ginchy ' ' Flers Courcelette," " Thiepval, Le Transloy " Ancre Heights, Ancre, 1916 "**Arras, 1917, '18,**" "Vimy 1917 " "Scarpe, 1917 18 ' ' Messines 1917 ' Pilckem ' ' Langemarck 1917,"" Menin Road ' Polygon Wood, " Broodseinde " Poelcappelle, " Passchendaele ' "**Cambrai, 1917, '18,**" ' St Quentin ' " Bapaume, 1918 ' ' " Rosières, ' " Lys, ' ' Estaires Hazebrouck Bailleul " Kemmel " ' Béthune ' " Tardenois ' ' Drocourt Quéant Hindenburg Line ' " Havrincourt, " Canal du Nord " ' Courtrai Selle ' ' Valenciennes ' Sambre ' " France and Flanders 1914–18 Italy 1917–18 Kosturino,' 'Struma,' "**Doiran, 1917, '18,**" ' Macedonia 1915–18 ' " Helles ' "**Landing at Helles,**" " Krithia, ' "**Suvla,**" Sari Bair ' " Landing at Suvla ' ' Scimitar Hill, ' "Gallipoli 1915–16 ' Egypt 1915–17 " "**Gaza,**" El Mughar ' Nebi Samwil ' Jerusalem, Jaffa " Tell Asur, " Megiddo," " Sharon ' Palestine, 1917–18." Aden " ' Shaiba "**Kut al Amara, 1915, '17,**" Tigris 1916 Baghdad ' Sharqat, " Mesopotamia, 1915–18." Persia 1918 19 ' Archangel 1919 ' " Siberia 1918–19

THE SOUTH STAFFORDSHIRE REGIMENT

THE GREAT WAR—18 Battalions

"**Mons,**" Retreat from Mons, "**Marne, 1914,**" "**Aisne, 1914, '18,**" "**Ypres, 1914, '17,**" Langemarck 1914 '17 " "Gheluvelt Nonne Bosschen, ' Neuve Chapelle, 'Aubers Festubert 1915 " "**Loos,**" "**Somme, 1916, '18,**" " Albert 1916 18, ' 'Bazentin,' 'Delville Wood ' 'Pozières 'Flers Courcelette 'Morval,' Thiepval, "Ancre 1916, ' ' Bapaume, 1917, '18 Arras, 1917 '18 ' 'Scarpe, 1917, '18 'Arleux " Bullecourt, "Hill 70 Messines 1917, 18 ' 'Menin Road Polygon Wood ' Broodseinde,' Poelcappelle "Passchen daele ' "**Cambrai, 1917, '18,**" "St Quentin ' 'Lys, Bailleul ' "Kemmel,' Scherpenberg Drocourt Quéant," ' Hindenburg Line "Havrincourt ' Canal du Nord ' "**St Quentin Canal,**" Beaurevoir Selle Sambre, "France and Flanders 1914–18 Piave ' "**Vittorio Veneto,**" Italy, 1917–18 " "**Suvla,**" Landing at Suvla ' Scimitar Hill,' "Gallipoli 1915 'Egypt 1916 "

THE DORSETSHIRE REGIMENT

THE GREAT WAR—13 Battalions

"**Mons,**" Le Cateau Retreat from Mons, "**Marne, 1914,**" "Aisne, 1914," ' La Bassée, 1914 Armentières 1914 ' "**Ypres, 1915, '17,**" Gravenstafel, St Julien,' Belle waarde ' "**Somme, 1916, '18,**" ' Albert 1916, 18 Flers Courcelette, 'Thiepval Ancre 1916 18, ' ' Arras 1917 ' "Scarpe 1917 ' Messines 1917 ' Langemarck 1917, Polygon Wood ' 'Broodseinde," Poelcappelle " 'Passchendaele "St. Quentin "Amiens " ' Bapaume 1918, "**Hindenburg Line,**" 'Épéhy Canal du Nord ' 'St Quentin Canal '' Beaurevoir Cambrai 1918 " ' Selle " "**Sambre,**" ' France and Flanders, 1914–18 "**Suvla,**" Landing at Suvla 'Scimitar Hill " Gallipoli 1915 Egypt 1916." "**Gaza,**" El Mughar Nebi Samwil, Jerusalem, Tell 'Asur ' 'Megiddo ' Sharon Palestine 1917–18 ' ' Basra, ' "**Shaiba,**" "Kut al Amara, 1915 17 "**Ctesiphon,**" 'Defence of Kut al Amara " ' Baghdad Mesopotamia 1914–18 "

THE PRINCE OF WALES'S VOLUNTEERS (SOUTH LANCASHIRE)

THE GREAT WAR—20 Battalions

"**Mons**," Le Cateau, ' Retreat from Mons, ' Marne 1914, "**Aisne, 1914, '18,**" "La Bassée, 1914 ' "**Messines, 1914, '17, '18,**" "Armentières 1914 " "**Ypres, 1914, '15, '17, '18,**" ' Nonne Bosschen ' "St Julien ' Frezenberg " ' Bellewaarde "**Somme, 1916, '18,**" Albert 1916 ' "Bazentin, ' "Pozières, Guillemont ' ' Ginchy, " Flers Courcelette ' " Morval," " Le Transloy ' ' Ancre Heights ' Ancre, 1916 " Arras, 1917, 18, ' ' Scarpe 1917 '18 ' " Pilckem, ' " Langemarck, 1917,' " Menin Road " ' Polygon Wood,' " Passchendaele, ' Cambrai, 1917, '18," St Quentin ' Bapaume, 1918 " ' Rosières " "**Lys,**" ' Estaires " Hazebrouck," ' Bailleul ' Kemmel, ' Scherpenberg,' " Drocourt Quéant ' Hindenburg Line " Canal du Nord ' Courtrai, " Selle, ' Sambre " " France and Flanders, 1914–18. "**Doiran, 1917, '18,**" Macedonia 1915–18 " ' Suvla ' "**Sari Bair,**" " Gallipoli 1915 ' " Egypt 1916 Tigris 1916, ' Kut al Amara 1917,' "**Baghdad,**" Mesopotamia 1916–18 "**Baluchistan, 1918** "

THE WELCH REGIMENT

THE GREAT WAR—34 Battalions

Mons, Retreat from Mons, Marne 1914 "**Aisne, 1914, '18,**" "**Ypres, 1914, '15, '17,**" "Langemarck 1914, 17 " "**Gheluvelt,**" ' Nonne Bosschen ' Givenchy 1914, ' ' Gravenstafel ' ' St Julien ' Frezenberg, ' Bellewaarde," Aubers ' ' Loos, "**Somme, 1916, '18,**" ' Albert 1916 '18 " Bazentin Pozières ' ' Flers Courcelette " Morval, ' Ancre Heights, Ancre 1916 18 ' ' Messines 1917 '18 ' "**Pilckem,**" " Menin Road ' " Polygon Wood ' Broodseinde,' Poelcappelle " " Passchendaele,' "**Cambrai, 1917, '18,**" St Quentin Bapaume, 1918, Lys ' Estaires ' ' Hazebrouck Bailleul Kemmel,' " Béthune, " Scherpenberg,' " Arras, 1918, Drocourt Quéant ' " Hindenburg Line,' " Épéhy " " St. Quentin Canal ' ' Beaurevoir ' " Selle ' Valenciennes ' Sambre," " France and Flanders, 1914–18 Struma " " Doiran 1917 18," "**Macedonia, 1915–18** " Suvla " " Sari Bair," " Landing at Suvla,' " Scimitar Hill "**Gallipoli, 1915** " " Egypt 1915–17 " " Gaza ' " El Mughar, ' " Jerusalem," Jericho ' ' Tell 'Asur, Megiddo " Nablus,' "**Palestine, 1917–18** " Tigris 1916,' Kut al Amara 1917 ' Baghdad ' "**Mesopotamia, 1916 18** "

THE BLACK WATCH (ROYAL HIGHLANDERS)

THE GREAT WAR—25 Battalions

Retreat from Mons **"Marne, 1914, '18,"** Aisne 1914, La Bassée 1914 ' **"Ypres, 1914, '17, '18,"** Langemarck, 1914 ' "Gheluvelt, 'Nonne Bosschen' "Givenchy 1914 " ' Neuve Chapelle" Aubers 'Festubert, 1915 ' **"Loos," "Somme, 1916, '18,"** ' Albert 1916," "Bazentin, Delville Wood," "Pozières, "Flers Courcelette' Morval ' Thiepval,' ' Le Transloy" ' Ancre Heights,' "Ancre 1916 ' **"Arras, 1917, '18,"** "Vimy, 1917, ' Scarpe, 1917 '18, ' Arleux " "Pilckem ' 'Menin Road 'Polygon Wood ' Poelcappelle Passchendaele " Cambrai 1917, '18 ' "St. Quentin," ' Bapaume 1918 "Rosières **"Lys,"** ' Estaires, ' Messines, 1918 "'"Hazebrouck Kemmel Béthune," ' Scherpenberg " ' Soissonnais Ourcq ' Tardenois, Drocourt Quéant, **"Hindenburg Line,"** "Épéhy St Quentin Canal, '"Beaurevoir 'Courtrai '"Selle,' Sambre France and Flanders, 1914–18 ' **"Doiran, 1917,"** ' Macedonia, 1915–18 "Egypt 1916 ' Gaza ' 'Jerusalem Tell Asur " **"Megiddo,"** "Sharon Damascus ' "Palestine, 1917–18 ' Tigris 1916 **"Kut al Amara, 1917,"** ' Baghdad Mesopotamia 1915 17 '

THE OXFORDSHIRE AND BUCKINGHAMSHIRE LIGHT INFANTRY

THE GREAT WAR—17 Battalions

"Mons," Retreat from Mons ' Marne 1914, Aisne, 1914 **"Ypres, 1914, '17,"** **"Langemarck, 1914, '17,"** ' Gheluvelt **"Nonne Bosschen,"** ' Aubers," "Festubert, 1915, ' "Hooge 1915 " "Loos ' "Mount Sorrel " **"Somme, 1916, '18,"** Albert 1916, 18 ' "Bazentin ' 'Delville Wood,' "Pozières Guillemont ' Flers Courcelette," "Morval " "Le Transloy Ancre Heights ' Ancre, 1916 ' Bapaume, 1917 18 ' "Arras 1917 ' "Vimy 1917 ' ' Scarpe 1917 ' "Arleux ' Menin Road Polygon Wood "Broodseinde, Poelcappelle,' "Passchendaele ' **"Cambrai, 1917, '18,"** St Quentin ' Rosières ' "Avre Lys," "Hazebrouck "' Béthune ' ' Hindenburg Line Havrincourt,' Canal du Nord' "Selle ' "Valenciennes France and Flanders, 1914–18. ' **"Piave,"** Vittorio Veneto Italy 1917–18 ' **"Doiran, 1917, '18,"** "Macedonia 1915–18 Kut al Amara, 1915, ' **"Ctesiphon," "Defence of Kut al Amara,"** "Khan Baghdadi " "Mesopotamia 1914–18 "Archangel 1919 "

THE ESSEX REGIMENT

THE GREAT WAR—31 Battalions

"**Le Cateau,**" Retreat from Mons, "**Marne, 1914,**" 'Aisne 1914,' ' Messines, 1914 " Armentières 1914 " "**Ypres, 1915, '17,**" St Julien,' Frezenberg,' ' Bellewaarde ' "**Loos,**" "**Somme, 1916, '18,**" " Albert 1916 18, " Bazen tin, ' "Delville Wood, Pozières, Flers Courcelette ' Morval,' " Thiepval Le Transloy, "Ancre Heights " " Ancre, 1916 18,' ' Bapaume 1917, '18, "**Arras, 1917, '18,**" ' Scarpe 1917, 18 ' ' Arleux,' "Pilckem, "Langemarck, 1917 ' Menin Road Broodseinde,' " Poelcappelle,' " Passchendaele ' "**Cambrai, 1917, '18,**" St Quentin,' Avre " " Villers Bretonneux, ' Lys, Hazebrouck " Béthune ' Amiens ' ' Drocourt Quéant ' ' Hindenburg Line, Havrincourt 'Épéhy St Quentin Canal "**Selle,**" " Sambre ' " France and Flanders, 1914–18 " ' Helles Landing at Helles, ' Krithia " ' Suvla " ' Landing at Suvla ' Scimitar Hill " "**Gallipoli, 1915–16 **" Rumani, ' Egypt 1915–17.'' "**Gaza,**" " Jaffa ' Megiddo Sharon " Palestine 1917–18

THE SHERWOOD FORESTERS (NOTTINGHAMSHIRE AND DERBYSHIRE REGIMENT)

THE GREAT WAR—30 Battalions

"**Aisne, 1914, '18,**" Armentières 1914, "**Neuve Chapelle,**" Aubers ' "Hooge 1915 " "**Loos,**" "**Somme, 1916, '18,**" Albert 1916 '18 ' Bazentin," ' Delville Wood, Pozières, Ginchy ' ' Flers Courcelette ' Morval ' Thiepval," " Le Transloy Ancre Heights," ' Ancre, 1916 Arras 1917, 18 ' " Vimy, 1917 " " Scarpe, 1917 '18 ' ' Messines, 1917 "**Ypres, 1917, '18,**" Pilckem,' ' Langemarck, 1917 " " Menin Road ' " Polygon Wood ' " Broodseinde " Poelcappelle ' " Passchen daele ' "**Cambrai, 1917, '18,**" " St. Quentin," " Bapaume 1918 ' ' Rosières ' " Villers Bretonneux " Lys ' " Bailleul ' " Kemmel Scherpenberg Amiens " Drocourt Quéant ' Hindenburg Line, ' 'Épéhy, Canal du Nord ' "**St. Quentin Canal,**" " Beau revoir ' Courtrai ' " Selle ' ' Sambre," "**France and Flanders, 1914–18.**" " Piave, "**Italy, 1917–18 **" ' Suvla " " Landing at Suvla ' Scimitar Hill "**Gallipoli, 1915 **" ' Egypt 1916 '

THE LOYAL REGIMENT (NORTH LANCASHIRE)

THE GREAT WAR—21 Battalions

"**Mons**," Retreat from Mons, Marne, 1914 18 "**Aisne, 1914, '18**," "**Ypres, 1914, '17, '18**," " Langemarck 1914 ' "Gheluvelt Nonne Bosschen,' Givenchy 1914,' "Aubers Festubert, 1915 " "Loos "**Somme, 1916, '18**," Albert, 1916 ' "Bazentin, "Pozières "Guillemont ' Ginchy " Flers Courcelette,' Morval '"Ancre Heights, Ancre 1916 Arras 1917, '18 ' Scarpe, 1917 ' ' Arleux "' Messines 1917 Pilckem ' ' Menin Road," Polygon Wood Poelcappelle Passchendaele "'Cambrai, 1917 18 ' "St. Quentin,' ' Bapaume, 1918 ' "**Lys**," Estaires " "Bailleul ' Kemmel ' Béthune ' Scherpenberg ' Soissonnais Ourcq "Drocourt Quéant, "**Hindenburg Line**," "Épéhy, ' ' Canal du Nord " "St Quentin Canal," "Courtrai ' ' Selle," "Sambre " "France and Flanders, 1914–18 "Doiran, 1917, ' Macedonia, 1917. "**Suvla**," ' Sari Bair "Gallipoli, 1915.' "Egypt, 1916 "**Gaza**," Nebi Samwil "Jerusalem, '"Jaffa "" Tell 'Asur, Palestine, 1917–18 '" Tigris, 1916," "Kut al Amara 1917,' "**Baghdad**," ' Mesopotamia 1916-18 "**Kilimanjaro**," E Africa 1914-16 "

THE NORTHAMPTONSHIRE REGIMENT

THE GREAT WAR—13 Battalions

"**Mons**," Retreat from Mons, "**Marne, 1914**," "**Aisne, 1914, '18**," "**Ypres, 1914, '17**," Langemarck 1914, 17 ' "Gheluvelt . Nonne Bosschen, Givenchy, 1914, "**Neuve Chapelle**,"' Aubers " "**Loos**," "**Somme, 1916, '18**," Albert 1916 '18, Bazentin "Delville Wood,' "Pozières ' Flers Courcelette, "Morval, Thiepval "Le Transloy, Ancre Heights,' "Ancre 1916, 18 ' Bapaume 1917, '18,' "**Arras, 1917,'18**," 'Vimy 1917 ' ' Scarpe 1917 18 ' 'Arleux,' Messines 1917 ' "Pilckem,' ' Passchendaele, ' "Cambrai 1917, 18 " ' St. Quentin '"Rosières ' "Avre ' "Villers Bretonneux " Amiens "

Drocourt Quéant, Hindenburg Line "**Épéhy**," St Quentin Canal, ' ' Selle " ' Sambre "France and Flanders, 1914–18 " ' Suvla, 'Landing at Suvla ' Scimitar Hill "Gallipoli 1915 Egypt, 1915-17 " "**Gaza**," El Mughar Nebi Samwil Jerusalem ' ' Jaffa ' Tell Asur "Megiddo ' Sharon Palestine 1917–18

THE ROYAL BERKSHIRE REGIMENT (PRINCESS CHARLOTTE OF WALES'S)

THE GREAT WAR – 16 Battalions

"**Mons**," Retreat from Mons Marne, 1914, Aisne 1914, '18 " " **Ypres, 1914, '17,**" Langemarck 1914 17, Gheluvelt ' Nonne Bosschen ' "**Neuve Chapelle,**" ' Aubers ' Festubert 1915 " " **Loos,**" " **Somme, 1916, '18,**" " Albert 1916 18,' ' Bazentin, ' Delville Wood ' Pozières, Flers Courcelette, Morval, Thiepval ' "Le Transloy,' Ancre Heights,' ' Ancre 1916, 18 " " **Arras, 1917, '18,**" Scarpe 1917, 18, ' Arleux,' " Pilckem ' ' Polygon Wood Broodseinde,' ' Poelcappelle Passchendaele ' " **Cambrai, 1917, '18,**" ' St Quentin " ' Bapaume 1918 " ' Rosières ' " Avre, ' Villers Bretonneux " Lys " Hazebrouck,' Béthune, ' Amiens ' " Hindenburg Line " Havrincourt, ' ' Épéhy " " Canal du Nord St Quentin Canal " **Selle,**" Valenciennes, ' Sambre France and Flanders, 1914–18. ' Piave " **Vittorio Veneto,**" Italy 1917–18 " " **Doiran, 1917, '18,**" Macedonia 1915–18

THE QUEEN'S OWN ROYAL WEST KENT REGIMENT

THE GREAT WAR– 18 Battalions

"**Mons,**" ' Le Cateau, Retreat from Mons, Marne 1914 Aisne, 1914, " La Bassée, 1914,' " Messines 1914, 17,' " **Ypres, 1914, '15, '17, '18,**" " **Hill 60,**" ' Gravenstafel ' " St Julien ' " Frezenberg ' Loos, " **Somme, 1916, '18,**" Albert 1916, 18,' ' Bazentin ' " Delville Wood, ' Pozières Guillemont ' ' Flers Courcelette, ' Morval,' " Thiepval ' Le Transloy Ancre Heights ' Ancre 1916 18,' " Arras 1917 18 ' " **Vimy, 1917,**" " Scarpe 1917 ' ' Oppy ' Pilckem ' Langemarck, 1917 ' Menin Road, Polygon Wood Broodseinde," ' Passchendaele ' Cambrai 1917, 18,' St Quentin ' Rosières Avre ' " Villers Bretonneux,"' Lys ' Hazebrouck Kemmel Amiens " Bapaume, 1918 ' Hindenburg Line ' Épéhy Canal du Nord " ' St Quentin Canal " " Courtrai " Selle Sambre ' France and Flanders 1914–18 " **Italy, 1917–18** " Suvla ' Landing at Suvla Scimitar Hill,' " **Gallipoli, 1915** " Rumani,' Egypt, 1915–16 " " **Gaza,**" El Mughar ' Jerusalem " ' Jericho " ' Tell Asur " Palestine 1917–18 " **Defence of Kut al Amara,**" " **Sharqat,**" Mesopotamia 1915–18 '

THE KING'S OWN YORKSHIRE LIGHT INFANTRY

THE GREAT WAR—26 Battalions

Mons, "**Le Cateau,**" Retreat from Mons "**Marne, 1914, '18,**" Aisne 1914 18, ' I a Bassée, 1914," "**Messines, 1914, '17, '18,**" "**Ypres, 1914, '15, '17, '18,**" ' Hill 60 ' "Gravenstafel" St Julien "Frezenberg, "Bellewaarde, Hooge, 1915, "Loos ' "**Somme, 1916, '18,**" Albert 1916, 18, ' "Bazentin, "Delville Wood ' "Pozières, Guillemont ' 'Flers Courcelette, "Morval," 'Le Transloy " Ancre, 1916, Arras 1917 18 " Scarpe 1917 ' "Langemarck 1917," ' Menin Road " ' Polygon Wood Broodseinde Poelcappelle " ' Passchendaele," "**Cambrai, 1917, '18,**" St. Quentin Bapaume, 1918 Lys " " Hazebrouck ' Bailleul " " Kemmel Scherpenberg," Tardenois "Amiens "Hindenburg Line, "**Havrincourt,**" Épéhy," Canal du Nord " "St. Quentin Canal "Beaurevoir " "Selle, ' 'Valenciennes, "**Sambre,**" 'France and Flanders 1914–18 ' Piave ' "Vittorio Veneto "**Italy, 1917–18 **" "Struma "**Macedonia, 1915–17 **" Egypt 1915–16 '

THE KING'S SHROPSHIRE LIGHT INFANTRY

THE GREAT WAR— 13 Battalions

Aisne 1914, 18 "**Armentières, 1914,**" "**Ypres, 1915, '17,**" Gravenstafel,' ' St Julien ' "**Frezenberg,**" "Bellewaarde Hooge, 1915,' Mount Sorrel "**Somme, 1916, '18,**" Albert 1916 '18, ' ' Bazentin, ' "Delville Wood ' ' Guillemont ' Flers Courcelette, ' Morval, Le Transloy, Ancre 1916 ' "**Arras, 1917, '18,**" Scarpe 1917," 'Arleux ' 'Hill 70, ' 'Langemarck, 1917 ' "Menin Road,' ' Polygon Wood ' Passchendaele ' "**Cambrai, 1917, '18,**" 'St Quentin " Bapaume, 1918 Rosières, ' Lys ' Estaires," Messines, 1918 ' "Hazebrouck Bailleul ' ' Kemmel " Béthune " "**Bligny,**" "Hindenburg Line "**Épéhy,**" Canal du Nord 'Selle, Valenciennes, "Sambre," 'France and Flanders 1914–18 " "**Doiran, 1917, '18,**" "Macedonia, 1915–18 ' "Gaza ' "**Jerusalem,**" 'Jericho ' 'Tell Asur " " Palestine 1917–18 '

THE MIDDLESEX REGIMENT (DUKE OF CAMBRIDGE'S OWN)

THE GREAT WAR—46 Battalions

" **Mons,**" Le Cateau, Retreat from Mons " **Marne, 1914,**" Aisne 1914 '18 " ' La Bassée 1914 ' Messines 1914 17, '18, ' Armentières, 1914, Neuve Chapelle " **Ypres, 1915, '17, '18,**" " Gravenstafel ' ' St Julien ' " Frezenberg, ' " Belle waarde ' Aubers," ' Hooge 1915 ' " Loos, ' Somme 1916, '18 ' " **Albert, 1916, '18,**" " **Bazentin,**" Delville Wood, ' ' Pozières, Ginchy " Flers Courcelette, ' Morval, ' ' Thiepval ' " Le Transloy, Ancre Heights,' ' Ancre 1916, 18," ' Bapaume 1917 '18 ' Arras 1917 '18 ' Vimy 1917 ' ' Scarpe, 1917 18 ' ' Arleux ' ' Pilckem, ' Langemarck, 1917 " " Menin Road ' Polygon Wood ' Broodseinde,' ' Poelcappelle " ' Passchendaele," " **Cambrai, 1917, '18,**" St Quentin Rosières ' " Avre, " Villers Bretonneux, ' Lys, ' Estaires Hazebrouck ' ' Bailleul " ' Kemmel, ' Scherpenberg " **Hindenburg Line,**" " Canal du Nord " ' St Quentin Canal Courtrai ' Selle, ' Valenciennes ' ' Sambre " " France and Flanders, 1914–18 ' Italy, 1917–18 " Struma ' " Doiran, 1918 ' " Macedonia 1915 18.' " **Suvla,**" Landing at Suvla " Scimitar Hill " Gallipoli 1915 ' Rumani, ' Egypt, 1915–17 Gaza " El Mughar ' " **Jerusalem,**" " Jericho, ' ' Jordan Tell 'Asur," ' Palestine, 1917–18 " **Mesopotamia, 1917–18** " Murman 1919 ' " Dukhovskaya Siberia 1918 19 '

THE KING'S ROYAL RIFLE CORPS

THE GREAT WAR—26 Battalions

" **Mons,**" Retreat from Mons " **Marne, 1914,**" Aisne, 1914 " " **Ypres, 1914, '15, '17, '18,**" ' Langemarck, 1914 '17 " ' Gheluvelt, ' ' Nonne Bosschen Givenchy 1914 ' ' Graven stafel," St Julien " ' Frezenberg ' Bellewaarde Aubers,' ' Festubert, 1915 ' Hooge, 1915,' ' Loos, ' " **Somme, 1916, '18,**" " Albert 1916 18 ' ' Bazentin " Delville Wood, ' ' Pozières, ' Guillemont ' Flers Courcelette, Morval ' Le Transloy " Ancre Heights ' Ancre 1916 '18 " **Arras, 1917, '18,**" " Scarpe, 1917," " Arleux " " **Messines, 1917, '18,**" Pilckem " Menin Road ' " Polygon Wood " ' Broodseinde, Poelcappelle, " Passchendaele," " Cambrai, 1917 '18," " St. Quentin ' " Rosières " Avre," ' Lys ' Bailleul, ' Kemmel " ' Béthune " Bapaume 1918 " Drocourt Quéant " Hindenburg Line Havrincourt " **Épéhy,**" " **Canal du Nord,**" St. Quentin Canal," Beaurevoir ' " Courtrai " **Selle,**" " **Sambre,**" ' France and Flanders 1914–18 " Italy 1917–18 Macedonia 1916–18

THE WILTSHIRE REGIMENT (DUKE OF EDINBURGH'S)

THE GREAT WAR—12 Battalions

"**Mons,**" Le Cateau   Retreat from Mons   Marne, 1914, Aisne, 1914 '18 ' ' La Bassée 1914,' "**Messines, 1914, '17, '18,**" "Armentières 1914, "**Ypres, 1914, '17,**" "Langemarck 1914   Nonne Bosschen ' Neuve Chapelle,' Aubers,"' "Festubert, 1915 ' Loos,' "**Somme, 1916, '18,**" "Albert, 1916, 18" Bazentin "Pozières, Le Transloy" Ancre Heights " 'Ancre 1916 ' "**Arras, 1917,**" Scarpe 1917, 'Pilckem Menin Road, Polygon Wood,' Broodseinde ' 'Poelcappelle Passchendaele, St. Quentin " Lys, ' Bailleul ' ' Kemmel Scherpenberg ' "**Bapaume, 1918,**" "Hindenburg Line Épéhy " ' Canal du Nord "St Quentin Canal Beaurevoir Cambrai 1918 ' Selle, Sambre France and Flanders, 1914 18 ' Doiran, 1917,' "**Macedonia, 1915–18** " "Suvla " ' Sari Bair "**Gallipoli, 1915–16** " "Gaza, Nebi Samwil Jerusalem, Megiddo " "Sharon "**Palestine, 1917–18** " Tigris 1916 "Kut al Amara 1917 ' "**Baghdad,**" Mesopotamia 1916–18 '

THE MANCHESTER REGIMENT

THE GREAT WAR—42 Battalions

"**Mons,**" Le Cateau, Retreat from Mons   Marne 1914 Aisne 1914, ' La Bassée, 1914, "Armentières, 1914 "**Givenchy, 1914,**" Neuve Chapelle ' "**Ypres, 1915, '17, '18,**" Gravenstafel 'St. Julien,' 'Frezenberg, "Bellewaarde Aubers " "**Somme, 1916, '18,**" Albert, 1916, 18 ' Bazentin Delville Wood, "Guillemont,' Flers Courcelette, Thiepval, Le Transloy ' Ancre Heights Ancre 1916 18,' Arras, 1917, 18 ' Scarpe 1917, ' Bullecourt "Messines 1917 ' Pilckem ' ' Langemarck 1917   Menin Road, ' Polygon Wood Broodseinde ' Poelcappelle "Passchendaele ' St Quentin ' ' Bapaume 1918, ' "Rosières "Lys ' ' Kemmel Amiens, "**Hindenburg Line,**" "Épéhy Canal du Nord St Quentin Canal " "Beaurevoir 'Cambrai, 1918, 'Courtrai,' 'Selle," 'Sambre "France and Flanders, 1914 18 "**Piave,**" Vittorio Veneto ' Italy, 1917 18 'Doiran, 1917 "**Macedonia, 1915–18** " "Helles, ' Krithia 'Suvla ' Landing at Suvla " "Scimitar Hill "**Gallipoli, 1915** " Rumani,' ' Egypt 1915–17" "**Megiddo,**" "Sharon Palestine, 1918. Tigris 1916 Kut al Amara 1917 " "**Baghdad,**" ' Mesopotamia 1916–18

THE NORTH STAFFORDSHIRE REGIMENT
(THE PRINCE OF WALES'S)

THE GREAT WAR—17 Battalions

Aisne, 1914 18 "**Armentières, 1914,**" Loos, "**Somme, 1916, '18,**" ' Albert 1916, 18 ' "Bazentin, "Delville Wood ' " Pozières, ' Guillemont" ' Ancre Heights, "Ancre; 1916, "**Arras, 1917,**" "Scarpe 1917," "Arleux" "**Messines, 1917, '18,**" "**Ypres, 1917, '18,**" "Pilckem," Langemarck 1917 ' ' Menin Road ' "Polygon Wood ' Broodseinde ' ' Poel cappelle ' Passchendaele ' Cambrai 1917 '18 " "St. Quentin ' " Bapaume, 1918," Rosières ' Avre ' Lys ' Bailleul, Kemmel, ' "Hindenburg Line, ' Havrincourt, Canal du Nord, "**St. Quentin Canal,**" Beaurevoir " ' Courtrai " "**Selle,**" "Valenciennes ' "Sambre " "France and Flanders, 1914–18 "Suvla " "**Sari Bair,**" ' Gallipoli 1915–16 " " Egypt 1916 ' "Tigris 1916," "**Kut al Amara, 1917,**" ' Baghdad ' ' Mesopotamia, 1916 18 ' Baku "Persia 1918 "**N W Frontier India, 1915 **"

THE YORK AND LANCASTER REGIMENT

THE GREAT WAR –22 Battalions

Aisne 1914, Armentières, 1914, "**Ypres, 1915, '17, '18,**" Gravenstafel ' St Julien ' ' Frezenberg ' ' Bellewaarde Hooge 1915, Loos "**Somme, 1916, '18,**" Albert 1916, Pozières,' ' Flers Courcelette ' "Morval " Thiepval, ' Le Transloy " Ancre Heights "Ancre 1916, Arras, 1917 '18 " Scarpe 1917 '18, Arleux Oppy "**Messines, 1917, '18,**" Langemarck 1917 Menin Road " Polygon Wood Brood scinde, "Poelcappelle,' "**Passchendaele,**" "**Cambrai, 1917, '18,**"' St Quentin " "Bapaume 1918 " "**Lys,**" Hazebrouck ' ' Bailleul "Kemmel ' "Scherpenberg ' Marne 1918 Tardenois, Drocourt Quéant "Hindenburg Line " "Havrin court ' "Épéhy "Canal du Nord, ' "**Selle,**" "Valenciennes,' " Sambre ' "France and Flanders 1914–18 ' "**Plave,**""Vittorio Veneto " ' Italy, 1917–18 " "Struma, "Doiran 1917 ' "**Macedonia, 1915–18.**" ' Suvla "Landing at Suvla ' ' Scimitar Hill " "**Gallipoli, 1915 **" Egypt 1916 '

THE DURHAM LIGHT INFANTRY

THE GREAT WAR –37 Battalions

" **Aisne, 1914, '18,**" Armentières 1914   " **Ypres, 1915, '17, '18,**" ' Gravenstafel, " St. Julien ' Frezenberg, ' Belle waarde ' " **Hooge, 1915,**" " **Loos,**" " **Somme, 1916, '18,**" Albert 1916 '18,' Bazentin, " Delville Wood " Pozières Guillemont,' ' Flers Courcelette, ' Morval ' " Le Transloy Ancre Heights, " **Arras, 1917, '18,**" " Scarpe 1917 Arleux Hill 70,' " **Messines, 1917,**" Pilckem " " Langemarck 1917 Menin Road " Polygon Wood ' Broodseinde, " Passchendaele " Cambrai 1917 '18, " St Quentin ' " Rosières, ' " **Lys,**" " Estaires, ' " Hazebrouck " Bailleul," Kemmel," ' Scherpenberg " Marne, 1918 ' " Tardenois," ' Bapaume 1918 " **Hindenburg Line,**" ' Havrincourt ' Épéhy " " Canal du Nord " St. Quentin Canal Beaurevoir, Courtrai " Selle," " **Sambre,**" ' France and Flanders, 1914–18 ' " Piave, " Vittorio Veneto Italy 1917–18 " ' Macedonia, 1916–18.' ' Egypt 1915–16 N W Frontier India 1915 1916–17 ' ' Archangel 1918–19 '

THE HIGHLAND LIGHT INFANTRY
(CITY OF GLASGOW REGIMENT)

THE GREAT WAR– 26 Battalions

" **Mons,**" Retreat from Mons, Marne 1914 Aisne 1914 " **Ypres, 1914, '15, '17, '18,**" ' Langemarck, 1914, 17 Gheluvelt, ' Nonne Bosschen ' Givenchy 1914, " Neuve Chapelle ' ' St Julien, " Aubers, Festubert 1915 ' " **Loos,**" " **Somme, 1916, '18,**" Albert 1916 '18 ' ' Bazentin Delville Wood ' " Pozières ' Flers Courcelette, ' Le Transloy " Ancre Heights ' Ancre, 1916 '18 " **Arras, 1917, '18,**" " Vimy 1917 ' ' Scarpe 1917 '18, ' Arleux " Pilckem Menin Road, Polygon Wood " Passchendaele, ' Cambrai, 1917 '18,' ' St Quentin," " Bapaume 1918," " Lys, " Estaires ' Messines 1918," ' Hazebrouck Bailleul, " Kemmel ' " Amiens ' " Drocourt Quéant " **Hindenburg Line,**" " Havrincourt " Canal du Nord ' " St Quentin Canal ' " Beaurevoir,' " Courtrai " Selle,' ' Sambre,' ' France and Flanders 1914–18 " " **Gallipoli, 1915–16** " Rumani " Egypt 1916 ' Gaza, El Mughar," " Nebi Samwil " Jaffa " **Palestine, 1917–18** " " Tigris 1916," " Kut al Amara 1917 " Sharqat " **Mesopotamia, 1916–18** " " Murman 1919 " " **Archangel, 1919** "

THE SEAFORTH HIGHLANDERS (ROSS-SHIRE BUFFS, THE DUKE OF ALBANY'S)

THE GREAT WAR – 19 Battalions

Le Cateau   Retreat from Mons   **"Marne, 1914, '18,"** Aisne, 1914,   'La Bassée 1914,   Armentières, 1914 Festubert, 1914, 15, "Givenchy, 1914, ' Neuve Chapelle **"Ypres, 1915, '17, '18,"** "St Julien ' ' Frezenberg,' ' Belle waarde " ' Aubers ' **"Loos," "Somme, 1916, '18,"** Albert 1916 '   Bazentin   "Delville Wood   "Pozières   ' Flers Courcelette, ' ' Le Transloy, "Ancre Heights ' "Ancre, 1916 ' **"Arras, 1917, '18," "Vimy, 1917,"** "Scarpe 1917, 18 Arleux   ' Pilckem,   Menin Road, ' Polygon Wood Broodseinde ' ' Poelcappelle ' Passchendaele " **"Cambrai, 1917, '18,"** "St Quentin,' ' Bapaume 1918 ' "Lys   Estaires " "Messines   1918 "   ' Hazebrouck "   "Bailleul '   Kemmel Béthune   ' Soissonnais Ourcq,"   Tardenois   Drocourt Quéant " ' Hindenburg Line,' "Courtrai," "Selle   **"Valenciennes,"** France and Flanders, 1914–18 '   Macedonia, 1917– 18 " ' Megiddo ' "Sharon " **"Palestine, 1918."**   " Tigris 1916   ' Kut al Amara 1917   **"Baghdad,"** "Mesopotamia 1915–18

THE GORDON HIGHLANDERS

———

THE GREAT WAR—21 Battalions

"Mons," "Le Cateau,"   Retreat from Mons   **"Marne, 1914, '18,"** Aisne 1914,   La Bassée 1914, 'Messines 1914,' "Armentières, 1914, ' **"Ypres, 1914, '15, '17,"** "Langemarck, 1914   "Gheluvelt,'   Nonne Bosschen ' ' Neuve Chapelle " ' Frezenberg " ' Bellewaarde, ' Aubers   Festubert, 1915 Hooge, 1915, **"Loos," "Somme, 1916, '18,"** ' Albert 1916, '18, ' Bazentin, ' Delville Wood, "Pozières   Guille mont   " Flers Courcelette ' Le Transloy   **"Ancre, 1916,"** **"Arras, 1917, '18,"** ' Vimy 1917, ' Scarpe 1917, 18 Arleux   ' Bullecourt   Pilckem ' "Menin Road ' 'Polygon Wood "   Broodseinde   "Poelcappelle,   " Passchendaele " **"Cambrai, 1917, '18,"**   St Quentin '   Bapaume, 1918 Rosières   'Lys   ' Estaires   "Hazebrouck " ' Béthune Soissonnais Ourcq   Tardenois   Hindenburg Line " "Canal du Nord, ' "Selle '   Sambre   "France and Flanders 1914–18 " "Piave ' **"Vittorio Veneto,"**   Italy 1917–18

THE QUEEN'S OWN CAMERON HIGHLANDERS

THE GREAT WAR—13 Battalions

Retreat from Mons, **"Marne, 1914, '18,"** **"Aisne, 1914,"** **"Ypres, 1914, '15, '17, '18,"** 'Langemarck, 1914' "Gheluvelt' Nonne Bosschen' 'Givenchy 1914' **"Neuve Chapelle,"** Hill 60 Gravenstafel St Julien Frezenberg "Belle waarde, Aubers, "Festubert 1915 **"Loos," "Somme, 1916, '18,"** "Albert, 1916, ' Bazentin, **"Delville Wood,"** "Pozières ' 'Flers Courcelette," Morval ' Le Transloy "Ancre Heights **"Arras, 1917, '18,"** 'Scarpe 1917" Arleux," 'Pilckem Menin Road '' Polygon Wood ' Poelcappelle '''Passchendaele St Quentin Bapaume 1918 "Lys ' "Estaires,' Messines 1918 ' Kemmel ' Béthune, Soissonnais Ourcq ' Drocourt Quéant "Hindenburg Line ' Épéhy "St Quentin Canal ' "Courtrai "Selle '"**Sambre**," 'France and Flanders 1914 18 Struma **"Macedonia, 1915-18 "**

THE ROYAL ULSTER RIFLES

THE GREAT WAR– 21 Battalions

"Mons," Le Cateau Retreat from Mons **"Marne, 1914,"** Aisne 1914 ' La Bassée 1914, Messines, 1914 17 18 Armentières, 1914 **"Ypres, 1914, '15, '17, '18,"** Nonne Bosschen ' **"Neuve Chapelle,"** ' Frezenberg Aubers **"Somme, 1916, '18,"** **"Albert, 1916,"** Bazentin Pozières Guillemont,' ' Ginchy Ancre Heights "Pilckem '"Lange marck, 1917' Cambrai, 1917," 'St Quentin, Rosières 'Lys ' "Bailleul, Kemmel ' **"Courtrai,"** "France and Flanders, 1914–18 ' Kosturino **"Struma,"** Macedonia 1915–17 " **"Suvla,"** Sari Bair '' Gallipoli, 1915 Gaza **"Jerusalem,"** Tell Asur "Palestine 1917 18

THE ROYAL IRISH FUSILIERS (PRINCESS VICTORIA'S)

THE GREAT WAR— 14 Battalions

"**Le Cateau**," Retreat from Mons "**Marne, 1914,**" Aisne 1914,' Armentières 1914, "**Ypres, 1915, '17, '18,**" Gravenstafel, ' St Julien ' Frezenberg ' "Bellewaarde "**Somme, 1916, '18,**" ' Albert, 1916,' ' Guillemont '"Ginchy Le Transloy,' "**Arras, 1917,**" ' Scarpe 1917," "**Messines, 1917, '18,**"' Langemarck, 1917 ' Cambrai, 1917 ' St Quentin ' "Rosières "**Lys,**"" Bailleul Kemmel,' "Courtrai, '"France and Flanders 1914–18 ' "Kosturino' "Struma," "**Macedonia, 1915–17**" "**Suvla,**" Landing at Suvla ' Scimitar Hill " "Gallipoli 1915 Gaza ' ' Jerusalem " Tell Asur Megiddo Nablus "**Palestine, 1917–18** "

THE CONNAUGHT RANGERS

THE GREAT WAR—6 Battalions

"**Mons,**" Retreat from Mons Marne 1914, "**Aisne, 1914,**" "**Messines, 1914, '17,**" " Armentières 1914 "**Ypres, 1914, '15, '17,**" Langemarck 1914 17 ' Gheluvelt, Nonne Bosschen,' "Festubert, 1914 ' Givenchy, 1914 " Neuve Chapelle ' St. Julien,' ' Aubers Somme 1916, 18 "**Guillemont,**" Ginchy ' "St Quentin, Bapaume, 1918 ' Rosières "Hindenburg Line, "**Cambrai, 1918,**" "Selle,' France and Flanders, 1914–18 ' "**Kosturino,**" 'Struma,' 'Macedonia 1915– 17 ' 'Suvla, 'Sari Bair "**Scimitar Hill,**" 'Gallipoli, 1915 ' Gaza ' Jerusalem ' Tell Asur,' "**Megiddo,**" "Sharon Palestine 1917–18 Tigris 1916 "**Kut al Amara, 1917,**" Baghdad ' Mesopotamia 1916 18

THE ARGYLL AND SUTHERLAND HIGHLANDERS (PRINCESS LOUISE'S)

THE GREAT WAR—27 Battalions

"**Mons**," "**Le Cateau**," Retreat from Mons, "**Marne, 1914, '18**," Aisne 1914," La Bassée, 1914, ' 'Messines, 1914 '18,' Armentières 1914,' "**Ypres, 1915, '17, '18**," " Gravenstafel, "St Julien,' ' Frezenberg,' 'Bellewaarde" Festubert, 1915 ' "**Loos**," "**Somme, 1916, '18**," "Albert 1916 '18 " ' Bazentin, ' "Delville Wood," "Pozières ' Flers Courcelette Morval " Le Transloy ' ' Ancre Heights ' "Ancre, 1916 "**Arras, 1917, '18**," "Scarpe 1917, 18 " " Aileux ' ' Pilckem Menin Road ' Polygon Wood " ' Broodseinde ' "Poelcappelle Passchendaele, "**Cambrai, 1917, '18**," St Quentin Bapaume, 1918 ' Rosières ' Lys,' ' Estaires, "Hazebrouck," ' Bailleul "Kemmel," "Béthune ' "Soissonnais Ourcq ' Tardenois, Amiens,' ' Hindenburg Line,' "Épéhy ' ' Canal du Nord," "St Quentin Canal," "Beaurevoir" Courtrai Selle ' Sambre ' France and Flanders 1914–18 "Italy 1917–18 "Struma, "**Doiran, 1917, '18**," "Macedonia, 1915–18 Gallipoli 1915–16." Rumani,' Egypt, 1916 " "**Gaza**," El Mughar ' ' Nebi Samwil "Jaffa " "Palestine 1917–18

THE PRINCE OF WALES'S LEINSTER REGIMENT (ROYAL CANADIANS)

THE GREAT WAR—7 Battalions

"**Aisne, 1914**," Armentières, 1914 "**Ypres, 1915, '17, '18**," Gravenstafel,' St Julien " ' Frezenberg ' "**Somme, 1916, '18**," "Delville Wood," "**Guillemont**," Ginchy' ' Arras, 1917 "**Vimy, 1917**," "**Messines, 1917**," Pilckem " ' Langemarck 1917' "**St Quentin**," Bapaume, 1918 Rosières ' Courtrai, France and Flanders 1914–18 Kosturino, Struma ' "**Macedonia, 1915-17**" "Suvla Sari Bair ' "**Gallipoli, 1915**" ' Gaza "**Jerusalem**," ' Tell Asur ' "Megiddo ' "Nablus Palestine 1917–18 '

THE ROYAL MUNSTER FUSILIERS

THE GREAT WAR—11 Battalions

"**Retreat from Mons,**" Marne 1914 Aisne 1914 "**Ypres, 1914, '17,**" ' Langemarck, 1914, 17, " Gheluvelt Nonne Bosschen, Givenchy, 1914 ' "**Aubers,**" "Loos Somme 1916, '18 Albert 1916 ' Bazentin,' Pozières "**Guillemont,**" ' Ginchy ' ' Flers Courcelette ' ' Morval Messines, 1917 Passchendaele ' "**St. Quentin,**" Bapaume, 1918 " " Rosières " Avre ' ' Arras 1918 " " Scarpe 1918 " "**Drocourt-Quéant,**" Hindenburg Line, Canal du Nord St Quentin Canal " Beaurevoir " ' Cambrai 1918, "**Selle,**" Sambre " " France and Flanders 1914–18 " ' Italy 1917–18 Kosturino " Struma ' ' Macedonia, 1915–17 ' ' Helles "**Landing at Helles,**" Krithia,' "Suvla "**Landing at Suvla,**" " Scimitar Hill, Gallipoli, 1915–16 Egypt, 1916 ' " Gaza " **Jerusalem,**" Tell 'Asur ' " Palestine 1917–18 '

THE ROYAL DUBLIN FUSILIERS

THE GREAT WAR – 11 Battalions

Le Cateau "**Retreat from Mons,**" "**Marne, 1914,**" Aisne 1914,' Armentières 1914, "**Ypres, 1915, '17, '18,**" St. Julien ' Frezenberg,' ' Bellewaarde "**Somme, 1916, '18,**" " Albert 1916, ' Guillemont "Ginchy ' Le Transloy ' Ancre 1916, "Arras 1917 " Scarpe 1917," Arleux Messines 1917, Langemarck, 1917 ' Polygon Wood "**Cambrai, 1917, '18,**" " St Quentin, Bapaume 1918 Rosières " Avre ' "**Hindenburg Line,**" St Quentin Canal Beaurevoir, Courtrai,' "**Selle,**" "Sambre,' ' France and Flanders 1914–18 ' "Kosturino ' Struma," "**Macedonia, 1915–17.**" ' Helles, Landing at Helles," "Krithia ' "Suvla," "Sari Bair, ' Landing at Suvla ' Scimitar Hill," "**Gallipoli, 1915–16 **" Egypt, 1916 ' " Gaza ' Jerusalem ' Tell 'Asur " "**Palestine, 1917–18 **"

THE RIFLE BRIGADE (PRINCE CONSORT'S OWN)

THE GREAT WAR—21 Battalions

"**Le Cateau,**" ' Retreat from Mons, "**Marne, 1914,**" Aisne 1914, 18," ' Armentières 1914, "**Neuve Chapelle,**" "**Ypres, 1915, '17,**" "Gravenstafel,' St Julien" "Frezenberg,' "Bellewaarde, Aubers ' "Hooge, 1915," "**Somme, 1916, '18,**" "Albert 1916 '18,' Bazentin ' ' Delville Wood "' Guillemont Flers Courcelette, ' "Morval Le Transloy Ancre Heights ' Ancre, 1916 18 "**Arras, 1917, '18,**" "Vimy, 1917 ' "Scarpe 1917 '18," Arleux "**Messines, 1917,**" "Pilckem, Langemarck 1917 "Menin Road ' "Polygon Wood ' ' Broodseinde ' "Poelcappelle "Passchendaele " "**Cambrai, 1917, '18,**" St Quentin,' "Rosières " Avre Villers Bretonneux ' 'Lys 'Hazebrouck Béthune Drocourt Quéant, ' "**Hindenburg Line,**" Havrincourt Canal du Nord "Selle "Valenciennes Sambre ' France and Flanders 1914–18 "**Macedonia, 1915–18** "

THE MONMOUTHSHIRE REGIMENT

THE GREAT WAR— 11 Battalions

"**Ypres, 1915, '17, '18,**" Gravenstafel, "**St Julien,**" Frezenberg,' 'Bellewaarde ' "**Somme, 1916,**" Albert 1916, "**Arras, 1917,**" "**Scarpe, 1917,**" "Pilckem "**Langemarck, 1917,**" "Poelcappelle ' "**Cambrai, 1917, '18,**" "Lys " "Messines 1918," "**Hindenburg Line,**" ' St Quentin Canal Beaurevoir,' "Courtrai "Sambre " "**France and Flanders, 1914 18** " "**Aden** "

THE CAMBRIDGESHIRE REGIMENT

THE GREAT WAR—4 Battalions

"**Ypres, 1915, '17,**" Gravenstafel St Julien Frezenberg ' "**Somme, 1916, '18,**" "Thiepval ' "**Ancre Heights,**" "Ancre 1916 " "**Pilckem,**" Menin Road "Polygon Wood, Broodseinde, ' Poelcappelle "**Passchendaele,**" ' St. Quentin "Rosières ' ' Lys " "**Kemmel,**" "Scherpenberg " "**Amiens,**" "Albert 1918 ' Bapaume 1918 "**Hindenburg Line,**" Épéhy, St Quentin Canal "**Pursuit to Mons,**" "**France and Flanders, 1915–18** "

1st CITY OF LONDON REGIMENT (THE ROYAL FUSILIERS)

THE GREAT WAR - 4 Battalions

Aubers "**Somme, 1916, '18,**" "**Albert, 1916, '18,**" Flers Courcelette "Morval,' Le Transloy' "**Arras, 1917, '18,**" "**Scarpe, 1917, '18,**" Bullecourt" "**Ypres, 1917,**" 'Langemarck 1917,' 'Menin Road," "Polygon Wood,' "Passchendaele," "**Cambrai, 1917,**" "**Hindenburg Line,**" Canal du Nord' Valenciennes' "Sambre' "**France and Flanders, 1915–18**" "**Gallipoli, 1915–16**" "**Egypt, 1916**"

2nd CITY OF LONDON REGIMENT (THE ROYAL FUSILIERS)

—

THE GREAT WAR—4 Battalions

"**Somme, 1916, '18,**" "**Albert, 1916, '18,**" Guillemont Ginchy" Flers Courcelette," "Morval, Le Transloy "**Arras, 1917, '18,**" Scarpe, 1917 18 '"**Bullecourt,**" "**Ypres, 1917,**" 'Langemarck, 1917" 'Menin Road '' Polygon Wood ' "Passchendaele ' "**Cambrai, 1917,**" "St Quentin,' Villers Bretonneux' "**Amiens,**" 'Bapaume, 1918" "**Hindenburg Line,**" "Épéhy '"Canal du Nord " "Valenciennes," "Sambre" "**France and Flanders, 1915–18**" "**Gallipoli, 1915–16**" Egypt 1915 16 '

3rd CITY OF LONDON REGIMENT (THE ROYAL FUSILIERS)

-- —

THE GREAT WAR 4 Battalions

"**Neuve Chapelle,**" Aubers, "**Festubert, 1915,**" "**Somme, 1916, '18,**" "**Albert, 1916, '18,**" Ginchy,' 'Flers Courcelette ' "Morval' Le Transloy ' "**Arras, 1917,**" "Scarpe 1917, "**Bullecourt,**" "**Ypres, 1917,**" "Langemarck 1917 ' Menin Road " "Polygon Wood ' "Passchendaele," "**Cambrai, 1917,**" St Quentin" Bapaume 1918," "**Villers Bretonneux,**" Amiens " Hindenburg Line, 'Épéhy "Pursuit to Mons France and Flanders 1915–18 "**Gallipoli, 1915**" ' Egypt 1915–16

4th CITY OF LONDON REGIMENT (THE ROYAL FUSILIERS)

THE GREAT WAR—4 Battalions

"**Neuve Chapelle**," "**Ypres, 1915, '17,**" St. Julien Aubers "**Festubert, 1915,**" "**Somme, 1916, '18,**" 'Albert, 1916 18 Guillemont '"Ginchy, 'Flers Courcelette' Morval" 'Le Transloy,' "**Arras, 1917, '18,**" "Scarpe 1917, 18 "**Bullecourt,**" Langemarck 1917," 'Menin Road,' Polygon Wood '"Passchendaele" "**Cambrai, 1917, '18,**" "St Quentin" Villers Bretonneux," Amiens," "Bapaume 1918' 'Hindenburg Line "**Canal du Nord,**" Valenciennes ' "**Sambre,**" "France and Flanders 1915–18 "**Gallipoli, 1915 16**" Egypt 1916

5th CITY OF LONDON REGIMENT (LONDON RIFLE BRIGADE)

THE GREAT WAR—3 Battalions

"**Ypres, 1915, '17,**" St Julien, 'Frezenberg "**Somme, 1916, '18,**" "**Albert, 1916,**" 'Guillemont, Ginchy, "Flers Courcelette Morval, "Le Transloy,' "**Arras, 1917, '18,**" "**Scarpe, 1917, '18,**" "**Bullecourt,**" Langemarck 1917 "**Menin Road,**" Polygon Wood Passchendaele, "**Cambrai, 1917,**" 'Hindenburg Line "**Canal du Nord,**" Valenciennes " 'Sambre "**France and Flanders, 1914 18**"

6th CITY OF LONDON REGIMENT (CITY OF LONDON RIFLES)

THE GREAT WAR—3 Battalions

'Festubert 1915 "**Loos,**" "**Somme, 1916, '18,**" Flers Courcelette,' "**Le Transloy,**" "**Messines, 1917,**" "**Ypres, 1917,**" "Menin Road,' Polygon Wood,' "**Passchendaele,**" "**Cambrai, 1917,**" "**St Quentin,**" 'Avre" "**Amiens,**" Albert 1918" Bapaume, 1918" "**Hindenburg Line,**" Epehy "Pursuit to Mons' 'France and Flanders 1915–18

7th CITY OF LONDON REGIMENT

THE GREAT WAR—3 Battalions

" **Festubert, 1915,**" " **Loos,**" Somme 1916, 18, " **Flers-Courcelette,**" " **Le Transloy,**" " **Messines, 1917,**" Ypres, 1917 ' " **Menin Road,**" Polygon Wood " **Passchendaele,**" " **Cambrai, 1917,**" ' Avre " **Villers Bretonneux,**" "**Amiens,**" Albert 1918, Bapaume 1918 " Hindenburg Line " Épéhy Pursuit to Mons ' France and Flanders 1915 18

8th (CITY OF LONDON) BATTALION, THE LONDON REGIMENT (POST OFFICE RIFLES)

THE GREAT WAR- 3 Battalions

" **Festubert, 1915,**" " **Loos,**" " **Somme, 1916, '18,**" Flers Courcelette, ' Le Transloy " **Bullecourt,**" " **Messines, 1917,**" " **Ypres, 1917,**" " Menin Road " Passchendaele, " **Cambrai, 1917,**" " **St Quentin,**" "**Amiens,**" Albert, 1918 Bapaume, 1918 ' Hindenburg Line,' " Épéhy ' " **Pursuit to Mons,**" France and Flanders 1915–18 '

9th LONDON REGIMENT (QUEEN VICTORIA'S RIFLES)

THE GREAT WAR—3 Battalions

" **Hill 60,**" " **Ypres, 1915, '17,**" Gravenstafel St Julien Frezenberg Bellewaarde, " **Somme, 1916, '18,**" ' Albert, 1916 '18 " Guillemont ' Ginchy,' " Flers Courcelette ' ' Morval Le Transloy, " **Arras, 1917,**" " **Scarpe, 1917,**" ' Langemarck, 1917, ' " Menin Road ' " Polygon Wood ' ' Passchendaele " " **Cambrai, 1917,**" " Bapaume 1918,' " **Villers Bretonneux,**" " **Amiens,**" " **Hindenburg Line,**" Épéhy " Pursuit to Mons ' " **France and Flanders, 1914–18** "

10th LONDON REGIMENT (HACKNEY)

THE GREAT WAR—3 Battalions

" **Ypres, 1917,**" ' Menin Road   Polygon Wood   ' Passchen daele " " **Villers Bretonneux,**" " **Amiens,**" ' Somme 1918 ' " Albert 1918   " Bapaume 1918 " " **Hindenburg Line,**" " **Épéhy,**"   Pursuit to Mons,   France and Flanders 1917–18 " **Suvla,**"   Landing at Suvla '   Scimitar Hill ' " Gallipoli 1915   Egypt, 1915–17 ' " **Gaza,**" ' El Mughar   Nebi Samwil   Jerusalem " **Jaffa,**" " **Tell 'Asur,**" " Megiddo   " **Sharon,**" Palestine 1917–18 "

11th LONDON REGIMENT (FINSBURY RIFLES)

THE GREAT WAR—3 Battalions

" **Bullecourt,**" " **Ypres, 1917,**"   Menin Road   Polygon Wood,   ' Passchendaele ' " **France and Flanders, 1917–18.**"   Suvla   " **Landing at Suvla,**" " Scimitar Hill,   " **Gallipoli, 1915 **"   " **Egypt, 1915–17 **"   " **Gaza,**" ' El Mughar," Nebi Samwil   Jerusalem   " **Jaffa,**" " Tell Asur " " **Megiddo,**" " Sharon   " **Palestine, 1917–18 **"

12th LONDON REGIMENT (RANGERS)

THE GREAT WAR—3 Battalions

" **Ypres, 1915, '17,**"   Gravenstafel   " **St Julien,**" " **Frezenberg,**" " **Somme, 1916, '18,**" " **Albert, 1916, '18,**" 'Guillemont,' " **Ginchy,**"   Flers Courcelette,' ' Morval   ' Le Transloy, "Arras 1917 " " **Scarpe, 1917,**" " Langemarck 1917 " Menin Road " " Polygon Wood,' ' Passchendaele ' " **Cambrai, 1917,**"   Villers Bretonneux ' " **Amiens,**" " Bapaume 1918 "

Hindenburg Line, " **Épéhy,**"   Pursuit to Mons   France and Flanders 1914–18 '

13th LONDON REGIMENT (PRINCESS LOUISE'S KENSINGTON REGIMENT)

THE GREAT WAR—3 Battalions

"**Neuve Chapelle**," "**Aubers**," "**Somme, 1916, '18,**" Albert, 1916, '18,' ' Guillemont "' Ginchy "' Flers Courcelette, Morval,' ' Le Transloy ' "**Arras, 1917, '18,**" " Scarpe 1917 18,' "**Ypres, 1917,**" ' Langemarck, 1917 ' "**Cambrai, 1917, '18,**" Hindenburg Line,' "Canal du Nord Valenciennes ' 'Sambre " "France and Flanders 1914–18 ' "**Doiran, 1917,**" Macedonia 1916–17 " "**Gaza,**" El Mughar "Nebi Samwil "**Jerusalem,**" ' Jericho ' "Jordan ' Megiddo ' "**Sharon,**" Palestine 1917–18 '

14th LONDON REGIMENT (LONDON SCOTTISH)

THE GREAT WAR—3 Battalions

"**Messines, 1914,**" "**Ypres, 1914, '17, '18,**" Gheluvelt Nonne Bosschen ' "**Givenchy, 1914,**" ' Aubers "**Loos,**" "**Somme, 1916, '18,**" ' Albert 1916 18 ' "Guillemont Ginchy ' "Flers Courcelette ' Morval ' Le Transloy "**Arras, 1917, '18,**" ' Scarpe 1917 18," Langemarck 1917 "**Cambrai, 1917, '18,**" "Hindenburg Line "Canal du Nord Courtrai ' "**Valenciennes,**" "Sambre " "France and Flanders, 1914–18. "**Doiran, 1917,**" Macedonia 1916–17 'Gaza " ' El Mughar, "Nebi Samwil "**Jerusalem,**" Jericho Jordan " "Tell Asur ' ' Palestine 1917–18 '

15th (COUNTY OF LONDON) BATTALION, THE LONDON REGIMENT (PRINCE OF WALES'S OWN, CIVIL SERVICE RIFLES)

THE GREAT WAR—3 Battalions

"**Festubert, 1915,**" Loos "**Somme, 1916, '18,**" "**Flers-Courcelette,**" "Le Transloy,' "**Messines, 1917,**" "**Ypres, 1917, '18,**" "**Cambrai, 1917,**" St Quentin "Ancre 1918 ' "Albert 1918,' "**Bapaume, 1918,**" "Amiens ' Courtrai France and Flanders, 1915–18 ' "Doiran 1917 Macedonia, 1916–17. "**Gaza,**" 'El Mughar Nebi Samwil "**Jerusalem,**" "**Jericho,**" Jordan Tell Asur "Palestine 1917–18 "

16th LONDON REGIMENT (QUEEN'S WESTMINSTER RIFLES)

THE GREAT WAR—3 Battalions

"**Hooge, 1915,**" "**Somme, 1916, '18,**" Albert, 1916, "Guillemont,' "Ginchy,' "Flers Courcelette, Morval ' 'Le Transloy," "**Arras, 1917, '18,**" 'Scarpe 1917, 18,' "**Ypres, 1917, '18,**" 'Langemarck 1917, "**Cambrai, 1917,**" Hindenburg Line "**Canal du Nord,**" 'Courtrai, "Valenciennes ' "**Sambre,**" France and Flanders, 1914–18 ' Doiran, 1917 "**Macedonia, 1916-17 ''** 'Gaza ' ' El Mughar, 'Nebi Samwil "**Jerusalem,**"' Jericho "**Jordan,**" "Tell Asur "Palestine 1917-18

17th LONDON REGIMENT (POPLAR AND STEPNEY RIFLES)

THE GREAT WAR—3 Battalions

Aubers "**Festubert, 1915,**" "**Loos,**" "**Somme, 1916, '18,**" "Flers Courcelette ' ' Morval Le Transloy ' "**Messines, 1917,**" "**Ypres, 1917, '18,**" ' Langemarck 1917, "**Cambrai, 1917,**" St Quentin,' ' Bapaume, 1918 'Ancre, 1918 ' "Albert 1918," Courtrai '' 'France and Flanders, 1915–18 ' "**Doiran, 1917,**" Macedonia 1916–17.' "**Gaza,**" ' El Mughar, ' "Nebi Samwil, "**Jerusalem,**" 'Jericho ' "**Jordan,**" " Tell Asur ' "Palestine, 1917–18 '

18th LONDON REGIMENT (LONDON IRISH RIFLES)

THE GREAT WAR—3 Battalions

Festubert, 1915 "**Loos,**" "**Somme, 1916, '18,**" Flers Courcelette ' "Morval LeTransloy '"**Messines,1917,**'"**Ypres, 1917,**" 'Langemarck 1917 ' "**Cambrai, 1917,**" ' St Quentin, ' "Bapaume, 1918 ' "Ancre 1918 ' 'Albert, 1918, 'Pursuit to Mons '' "**France and Flanders, 1915–18 ''** "**Doiran, 1917,**" ' Macedonia 1916-17 "**Gaza,**" ' El Mughar, "Nebi Samwil "**Jerusalem,**" 'Jericho "Jordan "**Palestine, 1917-18 ''**

19th LONDON REGIMENT (ST PANCRAS)

THE GREAT WAR— 3 Battalions

"**Festubert, 1915,**" "**Loos,**" Somme, 1916 18 Flers ' Courcelette, Morval Le Transloy ' "**Messines, 1917,**" Ypres 1917, Langemarck 1917 ' "**Cambrai, 1917,**" ' St. Quentin Bapaume 1918 " Ancre 1918 " "**Albert, 1918,**" "Pursuit to Mons " **France and Flanders, 1915–18** " ' Doiran, 1917 Macedonia 1916–17 ' ' Gaza ' ' El Mughar, "**Nebi Samwil,**" "**Jerusalem,**" Jericho " "**Jordan,**" "Megiddo ' " Sharon " **Palestine, 1917 18** "

20th LONDON REGIMENT (THE QUEEN'S OWN)

THE GREAT WAR—3 Battalions

"**Festubert, 1915,**" "**Loos,**" "**Somme, 1916, '18,**" Flers Courcelette, Morval ' Le Transloy,' "Messines, 1917 ' "**Ypres, 1917,**" ' Langemarck, 1917 ' "**Cambrai, 1917, '18,**" St. Quentin ' Bapaume, 1918 ' ' Ancre 1918 " Albert 1918 "**Hindenburg Line,**" ' Havrincourt " "Canal du Nord Selle," " Sambre France and Flanders, 1915–18 "**Doiran, 1917,**" Macedonia, 1916–17 "**Gaza,**" El Mughar, Nebi Samwil, "**Jerusalem,**" " Jericho " ' Jordan ' "**Palestine, 1917–18** "

21st LONDON REGIMENT (FIRST SURREY RIFLES)

THE GREAT WAR—3 Battalions

Aubers "**Festubert, 1915,**" "**Loos,**" "**Somme, 1916, '18,**" ' Flers Courcelette ' ' Le Transloy ' "**Messines, 1917,**" ' Ypres 1917 ' "**Cambrai, 1917,**" "St Quentin,' "**Bapaume, 1918,**" Ancre 1918 "Amiens "**Albert, 1918,**" ' Pursuit to Mons ' France and Flanders 1915–18 ' Doiran, 1917 ' "Macedonia 1916–17 " ' Gaza, El Mughar, Nebi Samwil "**Jerusalem,**" "**Jericho,**" "**Jordan,**" " Tell Asur " ' Palestine 1917–18 '

22nd LONDON REGIMENT (THE QUEEN'S)

THE GREAT WAR—3 Battalions

Aubers "**Festubert, 1915,**" "**Loos,**" "**Somme, 1916, '18,**" ' Flers Courcelette, ' Le Transloy, "**Messines, 1917,**" "**Ypres, 1917,**" "**Cambrai, 1917,**" ' St Quentin ' " Bapaume, 1918 ' " Ancre, 1918 "**Albert, 1918,**" " Pursuit to Mons " France and Flanders 1915–18 ' ' Doiran, 1917 ' ' Macedonia 1916–17. "**Gaza,**" ' El Mughar ' " Nebi Samwil,' "**Jerusalem,**" Jericho "**Jordan,**" Tell Asur ' " Megiddo ' Sharon Palestine 1917–18 '

23rd LONDON REGIMENT

THE GREAT WAR—3 Battalions

"**Festubert, 1915,**" "**Loos,**" "**Somme, 1916, '18,**" Flers Courcelette " " Le Transloy ' "**Messines, 1917,**" "**Cambrai, 1917,**" ' St Quentin ' Ancre, 1918 ' ' Albert 1918 ' Bapaume 1918,' "**Ypres, 1918,**" ' Courtrai ' " France and Flanders, 1915–18 ' Doiran 1917, "**Macedonia, 1916–17**" "**Gaza,**" El Mughar ' Nebi Samwil "**Jerusalem,**" " Jericho "**Jordan,**" Tell Asur ' Palestine 1917–18

24th LONDON REGIMENT (THE QUEEN'S)

THE GREAT WAR—3 Battalions

" **Aubers,**" "**Festubert, 1915,**" Loos Somme 1916, 18 "**Flers-Courcelette,**" Le Transloy ' "**Messines, 1917,**" Ypres 1917 "**Cambrai, 1917,**" " St Quentin ' "**Bapaume, 1918,**" ' Ancre 1918 " Albert 1918 " Hindenburg Line ' "**Épéhy,**" Pursuit to Mons France and Flanders, 1915–18 Doiran 1917 ' " Macedonia 1916–17 " "**Gaza,**" " El Mughar Nebi Samwil "**Jerusalem,**" Jericho "**Jordan,**" ' Tell Asur " Palestine 1917–18 '

25th (COUNTY OF LONDON) CYCLIST BATTALION, THE LONDON REGIMENT

THE GREAT WAR—3 Battalions

"**N W Frontier India, 1917**"

28th LONDON REGIMENT (ARTISTS' RIFLES)

THE GREAT WAR—2 Battalions

Ypres 1917 " Passchendaele," " Somme, 1918," St Quentin " " Bapaume, 1918," " Arras, 1918, ' " Ancre, 1918,' " Albert, 1918," " Drocourt-Quéant," " Hindenburg Line,' " Canal du Nord," " Cambrai, 1918," " Pursuit to Mons,' " France and Flanders, 1914–18 "

THE HERTFORDSHIRE REGIMENT

THE GREAT WAR—4 Battalions

" Ypres, 1914, '17," Nonne Bosschen " Festubert, 1915,' " Loos," " Somme, 1916, '18," Thiepval ' Ancre Heights " Ancre, 1916," " Pilckem," ' Menin Road, Polygon Wood Broodseinde, ' Poelcappelle Passchendaele " St Quentin,' Rosières,' ' Lys" " Kemmel, ' " Albert 1918, ' Bapaume 1918," " Hindenburg Line," " Havrincourt ' ' Cambrai, 1918 ' " Selle " Sambre," " France and Flanders, 1914–18 "

THE HEREFORDSHIRE REGIMENT

THE GREAT WAR—3 Battalions

Marne 1918 " Soissonnais-Ourcq," " Ypres, 1918,' " Courtrai," " France and Flanders, 1918 " Suvla " Landing at Suvla," ' Scimitar Hill ' " Gallipoli, 1915 " Rumani," Egypt 1916–17.' " Gaza," " El Mughar,' " Jerusalem," " Tell 'Asur," ' Palestine 1917–18

THE KENT CYCLIST BATTALION

THE GREAT WAR
" N W Frontier India, 1917 " " Baluchistan, 1918 "

THE WEST INDIA REGIMENT

THE GREAT WAR—2 Battalions

" Palestine, 1918 " " E Africa, 1916–18 " " Cameroons, 1915–16 "

THE BRITISH WEST INDIES REGIMENT

THE GREAT WAR—11 Battalions

Messines 1917 " Ypres, 1917," Polygon Wood Broodseinde ' ' Poelcappelle " Passchendaele,"" Pursuit to Mons," " France and Flanders, 1916–18 " " Italy, 1918 " Rumani " Egypt, 1916–17 " " Gaza," El Mughai, ' Nebi Samwil " Jerusalem," " Jaffa ' Megiddo " Nablus," " Palestine, 1917–18 "

WEST AFRICAN REGIMENT

THE GREAT WAR—1 Battalion

" Duala," " Cameroons, 1914–16 "

ROYAL JERSEY LIGHT INFANTRY (MILITIA)

THE GREAT WAR—4 Battalions

" The Great War "

ROYAL GUERNSEY MILITIA (LIGHT INFANTRY)

THE GREAT WAR—1 Battalions

" Ypres, 1917," " Passchendaele," " Cambrai, 1917," " Lys," " Estaires," " Hazebrouck," " France and Flanders, 1917–18 "

WEST AFRICAN FRONTIER FORCE :—
NIGERIA REGIMENT

THE GREAT WAR—9 Battalions

" Behobeho," " Nyangao," " E Africa, 1916–18 " " Duala,"
" Garua," " Banyo," " Cameroons, 1914–16."

GOLD COAST REGIMENT

THE GREAT WAR—5 Battalions

" Narungombe," " E. Africa, 1916–18 " " Kamina " " Duala,"
" Cameroons, 1914–16 "

SIERRA LEONE BATTALION

THE GREAT WAR—1 Battalion

" Duala," " Cameroons, 1914–16 "

GAMBIA COMPANY

THE GREAT WAR

Nyangao   E Africa 1917–18   Cameroons 1915–16

THE KING'S AFRICAN RIFLES

THE GREAT WAR—22 Battalions

" Kilimanjaro," " Narungombe," " Nyangao," " E Africa,
1914–18 "

INDEX

E

INDEX—*contd*

INDEX—*contd*

INDEX—*contd*

AMENDMENTS

Army Order 267 of July 1925

Additional honours granted and list revised for the following:

BEDFORDSHIRE YEOMANRY (LANCERS)

Somme, 1916, 18   Flers – Courcelette   Cambrai, 1917 18
 Amiens', Albert 1918', Hindenburg Line"   St Quentin
Canal' 'Beaurevoir' 'Pursuit to Mons"   France and
Flanders 1915-18"

ESSEX YEOMANRY (DRAGOONS)

Ypres 1915   St Julien   Frezenberg , Loos   Arras 1917
Scarpe 1917 , Somme, 1918" 'Amiens , Albert 1918
Hindenburg Line' "St Quentin Canal   Beaurevoir
Cambrai 1918 'Pursuit to Mons" France and Flanders
1914 18"

LEICESTERSHIRE YEOMANRY
(PRINCE ALBERT'S OWN) (HUSSARS)

Ypres 1914, 15   St Julien   Frezenberg , Arras 1917
Scarpe, 1917 "Amiens 'Hindenburg Line' Canal du Nord
Pursuit to Mons' "France and Flanders 1914 18'

NORTH SOMERSET YEOMANRY (DRAGOONS)

Ypres, 1914 15   Frezenberg , Loos , Arras 1917 , Scarpe
1917' 'Amiens'   Hindenburg Line" 'Beaurevoir', 'Cambrai
1918   Pursuit to Mons' "France and Flanders 1914 18'

Army Order 426 of November 1925

Choice of Colour Honour amended by the Buffs (East Kent
Regiment):

For Aisne, 1914 substitute **Aisne 1914   Armentièrs 1914**
substitute 'Armentièrs 1914

Army Order 8 of January 1927

Choice of Honour to be shown in Clarendon type in the Army List
amended by the Rifle Brigade (Prince Consort's Own):

For **Marne, 1914** substitute Marne 1914   France and
Flanders 1914 18 substitute **'France and Flanders 1914 18"**

Army Order 51 of March 1929

The Honour **Gallipoli 1915 16** substituted for **Gallipoli 1915**
by the Cameronians (Scottish Rifles)